Lecture Notes in Computer Scien

T0230540

Commenced Publication in 1973
Founding and Former Series Editors:
Gerhard Goos, Juris Hartmanis, and Jan van Leeuwen

Lecture Notes in Computer Science 4156

Sihem Amer-Yahia   Zohra Bellahsène
Ela Hunt   Rainer Unland
Jeffrey Xu Yu (Eds.)

Database and XML Technologies

4th International XML Database Symposium, XSym 2006
Seoul, Korea, September 10-11, 2006
Proceedings

 Springer

Volume Editors

Sihem Amer-Yahia
Yahoo! Research
New York, NY, 10011, USA
E-mail: sihem@yahoo-inc.com

Zohra Bellahsène
LIRMM UMR 5506 CNRS/Université Montpellier II
34392 Montpellier, France
E-mail: bella@lirmm.fr

Ela Hunt
Global Information Systems Group,
Institut für Informationssysteme, ETH-Zentrum
8092 Züich, Switzerland
E-mail: elahunt@inf.ethz.ch

Rainer Unland
University of Duisburg-Essen
Institute for Computer Science and Business Information Systems (ICB)
45117 Essen, Germany
E-mail: UnlandR@informatik.uni-essen.de

Jeffrey Xu Yu
The Chinese University of Hong Kong
Department of Systems Engineering and Engineering Management
Shatin, New Territories, Hong Kong, China
E-mail: yu@se.cuhk.edu.hk

Library of Congress Control Number: 2006931570
CR Subject Classification (1998): H.2, H.3, H.4, D.2, C.2.4

LNCS Sublibrary: SL 3 – Information Systems and Application, incl. Internet/Web
and HCI

ISSN   0302-9743
ISBN-10   3-540-38877-X Springer Berlin Heidelberg New York
ISBN-13   978-3-540-38877-7 Springer Berlin Heidelberg New York

Springer is a part of Springer Science+Business Media

springer.com

© Springer-Verlag Berlin Heidelberg 2006
Printed in Germany

Typesetting: Camera-ready by author, data conversion by Scientific Publishing Services, Chennai, India
Printed on acid-free paper   SPIN: 11841920   06/3142   5 4 3 2 1 0

Preface

The theme of the XML Database Symposium (XSym) is the convergence of database technology with XML technology. Since the first International XML Symposium in 2003, XSym has continued to provide a forum for academics, practitioners, users and vendors to discuss the use of and synergy between advanced XML technologies.

XSym 2006 received 32 full paper submissions. Each submitted paper underwent a rigorous review by independent referees. These proceedings represent a collection of eight excellent research papers. Their focus is on building XML repositories and covers the following topics: XML query processing, caching, indexing and navigation support, structural matching, temporal XML, and XML updates.

The organizers would like to express their gratitude to the XSym program committee for their efforts in providing very thorough evaluations of the submitted papers under significant time constraints. We also would like to thank Microsoft for their sponsorship and for the use of the Microsoft Conference Management Toolkit, and the local organizers, especially, Kyuseok Shim, for all they did to make XSym a pleasant and successful event.

July 2006

Sihem Amer-Yahia
Zohra Bellahsene
Jeffrey Xu Yu
Ela Hunt
Rainer Unland

Organization

General Chair

Zohra Bellahsene, LIRMM (France)

Local Chair

Kyuseok Shim, Seoul National University (Korea)

Program Committee Chairs

Sihem Amer-Yahia, Yahoo (USA)
Jeffrey Xu Yu, Chinese University of Hong Kong (China)

Proceedings

Rainer Unland, University of Duisburg-Essen (Germany)

Communications and Sponsorship

Ela Hunt, ETH Zurich (Switzerland)

Members of the International Program Committee

Ashraf Aboulnaga, University of Waterloo (Canada)
Bernd Amann, Université Paris 6 (France)
Denilson Barbosa, University of Calgary (Canada)
Omar Benjelloun, Stanford University (USA)
Veronique Benzaken, Université Paris-Sud (France)
Philip Bernstein, Microsoft Research (USA)
Philip Bohannon, Bell Laboratories - Lucent Technologies (USA)
Jihad Boulos, American University of Beirut (Lebanon)
Stephane Bressan, National University of Singapore (Singapore)
Yi Chen, Arizona State University (USA)
Alex Dekhtayar, University of Kentucky (USA)
Alin Deutsch, University of California at San Diego (USA)
Yanlei Diao, University of Massachusetts at Amherst (USA)
Irini Fundulaki, University of Edinburgh (UK)
Minos Garofalakis, Intel Research (USA)

Table of Contents

Kappa-Join: Efficient Execution of Existential Quantification in XML Query Languages

Matthias Brantner[1,*], Sven Helmer[2], Carl-Christian Kanne[1], and Guido Moerkotte[1]

[1] University of Mannheim, Mannheim, Germany
{brantner, kanne, moerkotte}@informatik.uni-mannheim.de
[2] Birkbeck College, University of London, London, United Kingdom
sven@dcs.bbk.ac.uk

Abstract. XML query languages feature powerful primitives for formulating queries, involving comparison expressions which are existentially quantified. If such comparisons involve several scopes, they are correlated and, thus, become difficult to evaluate efficiently.

In this paper, we develop a new ternary operator, called Kappa-Join, for efficiently evaluating queries with existential quantification. In XML queries, a correlation predicate can occur conjunctively and disjunctively. Our decorrelation approach not only improves performance in the conjunctive case, but also allows decorrelation of the disjunctive case. The latter is not possible with any known technique. In an experimental evaluation, we compare the query execution times of the Kappa-Join with existing XPath evaluation techniques to demonstrate the effectiveness of our new operator.

1 Introduction

Almost every XML query language features a construct that allows to express an existentially quantified comparison of two node-set valued subexpressions in a concise manner. Unfortunately, current XML query processors lack efficiency and scalability when facing such constructs [5,20]. The corresponding semantics resembles that of nested and correlated subqueries, which are notoriously difficult to evaluate efficiently. To illustrate this point, let us consider the following query: For hiring a teaching assistant, we search the database for a student who took an exam that was graded better than 'B'.

Here, both sides of the comparison in the where-clause are set-valued because there are many good students and students take more than one exam. The

for	$s	in	//student	
let	$best	:=	//exam[grade < 'B']/@id	
let	$exams	:=	$s/examination/@id	**Q1**
where	$exams = $best			
return	$s/name			

existential semantics of the XQuery general comparison operator requires that all students are returned which have at least one exam also contained in the set $best.

A naïve evaluation technique evaluates the steps in order of appearance. In Q1, this means to reevaluate the value of $best and $exams for every iteration of the for

---

* This work was supported by the Deutsche Forschungsgemeinschaft under grant MO 507/10-1.

S. Amer-Yahia et al. (Eds.): XSym 2006, LNCS 4156, pp. 1–15, 2006.

loop, and then check for an item that occurs in both sets. This is a wasteful strategy: A closer look at Q1 reveals that, in contrast to $exams, the value of $best does not depend on the value of $s, making the reevaluation of $best unnecessary. A common strategy in such cases is to move the evaluation of $best out of the for loop, and to materialize and reuse the result. However, this only alleviates the problem of repeated evaluation of the expression to which $best is bound. To answer the query, it is still necessary to evaluate the where-predicate, which is a correlated nested query due to the existential semantics of the '=' operator and the fact that it refers to variables from two scopes, the independent $best and the dependent $exams.

In this paper, we are concerned with an efficient evaluation of existentially quantified *correlation predicates* such as the where-clause of Q1. While this area has received some attention in the past [5,20], we show that, even in simple cases like our Query Q1, there is still unexploited optimization potential for typical query patterns in XML query languages. We propose the novel Kappa-Join operator that fits naturally into execution plans for quantified correlation predicates, is easy to implement and yet features a decorrelated evaluation algorithm.

Q1 is "simple" because the correlation predicate occurs "alone". What if the correlation predicates become more complex? Assume that we consider *either* good *or* senior students to be eligible for assistantship, as in the following query:

If the two clauses were combined with **and**, we could use techniques to decorrelate queries with correlation predicates that occur conjunctively. If the clauses were not correlation predicates, we could use techniques to improve performance for disjunctive predicates (e.g. Bypass operators [8]). However, there is no published technique to decorrelate *disjunctively* occurring correlation predicates.

```
for      $s        in    //student
let      $best     :=    //exam[grade < 'B']/@id
let      $exams    :=    $s/examination/@id          Q2
where    $exams = $best  or $s/semester>5
return   $s/name
```

Hence, we also present a Bypass variant of the Kappa-Join. This allows a decorrelated evaluation of disjunctively occurring correlation predicates, which has not been accomplished for any query language so far.

The main contributions of this paper are as follows:

- We introduce the novel ternary Kappa-Join operator that, while simple to implement, can efficiently evaluate complex correlated queries where the correlation predicate occurs conjunctively.
- We introduce a Bypass variant of the Kappa-Join that allows us to extend our technique to queries where the correlation predicate occurs in a disjunction.
- We provide experimental results, demonstrating the superiority of both the Kappa-Join and the Bypass Kappa-Join compared to other evaluation techniques.

The remainder of this paper is organized as follows. In the next section, we discuss basic concepts, such as dependency and correlation in XPath. In Sec. 3, we discuss the drawbacks of existing decorrelation approaches for XML query languages. Further, we introduce our novel Kappa-Join operator to efficiently evaluate queries with conjunctive correlation. Sec. 4 investigates the case of disjunctive correlation and presents the novel Bypass Kappa-Join. In Sec. 5 we experimentally confirm the efficiency of our approach. The last section concludes the paper.

2   XPath Query Processing

The problems discussed in the introduction affect most existing XML query languages. However, all of the involved issues occur even for the simple XPath language in its first version because it features nested predicates and existential semantics. In the following, we limit our discussion to XPath 1.0, because peripheral topics such as typing, query normalization, and translation into an algebraic representation can be presented in a simpler fashion for XPath than for the more powerful XQuery language. However, all of the techniques presented in this paper also apply for full-blown XQuery or similar languages, as long as they are evaluated algebraically (e.g. [23]). In fact, both queries from the introduction can be expressed in XPath syntax, as we will see below.

2.1   Normalization

The techniques presented in this paper are mainly developed to optimize comparison expressions with one dependent and one independent operand. To correctly identify such expressions, the first step of our normalization is to rewrite a predicate such that it consists of literals and the logic operators $\wedge$ and $\vee$. After normalization, each literal l consists either of a comparison or a negation thereof, i.e. l is of the form $e_1 \theta e_2$ or $\mathrm{not}(e_1 \theta e_2)$, where $\theta \in \{=, <, \leq, >, \geq, \neq\}$.

One example for "hidden" comparisons are location paths or other node-set valued expressions when used as Boolean expressions. In such cases, we make the node-set valued expression the argument of an auxiliary *exists* function and compare its result to true, which yields a regular binary comparison expression.

Further, to provide efficient evaluation for disjunctively occurring comparison expressions, the second step of our normalization separates literals occurring in a conjunction from those that occur disjunctively. To this end, we employ an operation for collecting all literals that occur conjunctively: A literal l occurs *conjunctively* in a predicate p_k if $p_k[\mathrm{false}]$ can be simplified to false. That is, if we replace all occurrences of l inside p_k by false, the repeated (syntactical) application of the Boolean simplification rules to eliminate Boolean constants simplifies $p_k[\mathrm{false}]$ to false.

2.2   Context Dependency and Correlation

In this paper, we are concerned with efficient evaluation of existentially quantified comparison expressions that are *correlated*. In general, correlation occurs when a variable of a nested scope is compared with a variable from an enclosing scope. XPath does not have variables that can be declared by the user, but we can define correlation in terms of XPath *contexts*, as follows.

Every XPath expression is evaluated with respect to a given context, which is a sequence of *context items*. For our discussion, it is sufficient to use a definition of context item that is slightly simpler than the original XPath context item. A context item is a tuple with three components: the *context node*, the *context position*, and the *context size*. In XPath, there is one global context, which must be specified as parameter of the evaluation process. The value of some constructs depends on *local contexts* that are generated by other subexpressions. The constructs that refer to the local context are location steps, relative location paths, and calls to `position()` and `last()`. We call these expressions *dependent* expressions. Expressions whose value is independent of the local context are called *independent* expressions.

If we apply this terminology to Queries Q1 and Q2 from the introduction, given in XPath syntax, we have

$$\underbrace{//\text{student}[\underbrace{\text{examination}/@\text{id}}_{\text{dependent}}}_{\text{independent}} = \underbrace{//\text{exam}[\text{grade} <' \text{B}']/@\text{id}]/}_{\text{independent}} \underbrace{\text{name}}_{\text{dependent}} \qquad \textbf{Q1}$$

$$//\text{student}[\underbrace{\text{examination}/@\text{id}}_{\text{dependent}} = \underbrace{//\text{exam}[\text{grade} <' \text{B}']/@\text{id}}_{\text{independent}} \text{ or } \underbrace{\text{semester}}_{\text{dependent}} > \underbrace{5}_{\text{indep.}}]/\text{name} \qquad \textbf{Q2}$$

We now can define the term correlation for XPath as used in the remainder of this paper: A comparison expression with two node-set valued operands one being dependent and one being independent is called *correlation predicate*, because it compares a local context and an enclosing context. All example queries presented in the introduction and above contain correlation predicates. A correlation predicate can occur both conjunctively and disjunctively. We call the former case *conjunctive correlation* and the latter *disjunctive correlation*. In Q1 there is only one comparison expression which is a special case of conjunctive correlation, i.e. one with only a single literal. Q2 is an example with disjunctive correlation. The second comparison expression is not a correlation predicate, because the operand 5 is not node-set valued.

3   Kappa-Join for Conjunctive Correlation

The key to an efficient evaluation of correlated queries is to avoid redundant computation, e.g. the evaluation of the inner independent expression. Such techniques are called decorrelation techniques and have been studied extensively in the context of relational and object-oriented systems [9,11,12,17,18,26]. Similar techniques have been proposed for the evaluation of XQuery and XPath [5,20]. One of them is an approach that applies decorrelation to existentially quantified comparison expressions [5]. However, this approach is suboptimal because unnecessary duplicates are generated and must be removed at the end of the evaluation.

The optimizations developed in this paper are presented in the form of algebraic operators. Hence, we need an algebra capable of evaluating XPath. We have chosen NAL as a perfect fit, since a translation from XPath to NAL is also available [4]. However, our approach is not limited to NAL and the translation of XPath into it. For example, our techniques are also applicable to other algebraic evaluation strategies such as [25].

At the beginning of this section, we describe our assumptions about algebraic translation and evaluation in more detail. For a more elaborate treatment of these topics, please refer to [4,5]. We then recapitulate the decorrelation approach from [5] and discuss its drawbacks. Afterwards, we introduce the novel Kappa-Join operator that features an efficient decorrelation algorithm avoiding these drawbacks.

3.1 Algebra and Translation

The universe of the NAL algebra for XPath 1.0 is the union of the domains of the atomic XPath 1.0 types (`string, number, boolean`) and the set of ordered sequences of tuples which represent XPath contexts. Each tuple represents one context node, position and size. Special attribute names are used to hold the context node (cn), the context position (cp) and the context size (cs).

The NAL algebra features well-known operators [4,20]. All the sequence-valued operators in the logical algebra have a corresponding implementation as an *iterator* [14] in the physical algebra. In the following, we primarily need the *Selection* σ, the *Projection* Π, the *Semi-Join* $\ltimes$, and the *D-Join* $\underset{\rightarrow}{\bowtie}$. All operators are described when they are needed for the first time. Additionally, they are formally defined in our technical report [21].

To convert XPath queries into algebraic expressions, we use the translation introduced in [4]. We briefly recapitulate the relevant part of the translation process by elaborating on the translation result for Q1 (see Fig. 1). However, we omit the translation of subexpressions that are orthogonal to our discussion and denote them by $\mathcal{T}[e]$, where e stands for any XPath expression. For instance, we denote the translation of the location path `//student` by $\mathcal{T}[//student]$. Its result is the sequence of context nodes produced by the location path.

For Q1 (see Fig. 1) the algebra expression provides a Selection (σ) for the only literal. In the subscript (denoted by a dashed line) of this Selection, there is an Aggregation operator ($\mathcal{A}$) that aggregates the input sequence into a singleton sequence with a single attribute by applying the aggregation function $exists$. It

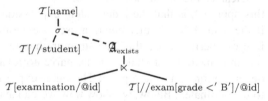

Fig. 1. Translation sketch for Q1

returns true if there exists at least one tuple in the input sequence. This input sequence stems from a Semi-Join ($\ltimes$), whose input sequences in turn stem from the two operands of the comparison expression, i.e. the two (translated) location path expressions. For a comparison between two node-sets, as in the particular case of Q1, we have an existential semantics. In the equality case, this fact can be leveraged by using a Semi-Join.

Because of the repeated evaluation of e_3 the worst-case complexity is $O(|e_1| \times |e_2| \times |e_3|)$ where $|e|$ denotes the cardinality of an expression e and, in this case, $e_1 = //student$, $e_2 = examination/@id$, and $e_3 = //exam\ldots$.

3.2 Existing Decorrelation Techniques

We now recapitulate the decorrelation approach introduced in [5] and discuss its drawbacks. Again, we take Query Q1 to illustrate this (see Fig. 1). The fundamental idea of decorrelation is to avoid unnecessary evaluations of an inner independent expression. In [5] this is achieved by pulling up the Semi-Join (see Fig. 1) into the top-level algebraic expression (see Fig. 2).

This expression needs some explanations. The dependent location path is connected to the outer expression using a D-Join ($\overrightarrow{\bowtie}$). The *D-Join* joins each tuple $t \in \mathcal{T}[//\text{student}]$ to all tuples returned by the evaluation of the dependent path $\mathcal{T}[\text{examination}/@\text{id}]$. For each t, $\mathcal{T}[\text{examination}/@\text{id}]$ is evaluated once, and free occurrences of variables in the dependent expression are substituted with the attribute values of t, i.e. the current context. At the end all resulting sequences are concatenated.[1]

The dependent expression, i.e. the evaluation using the D-Join, might produce duplicates for tuples from $\mathcal{T}[//\text{student}]$, hence the tid_A operator (tuple identifier) is needed to identify the tuples resulting from the outer expression.

The idea is to densely number the tuples, store this number in an attribute A, and use it later on to perform a duplicate elimination. To do this, we introduce an order-preserving duplicate elimination projection Π^{tid_A}, which removes multiple occurrences of the same tid-value A. It keeps the first tuple for a given A value and throws away the remaining tuples with the same value for A.

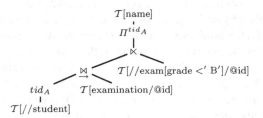

Fig. 2. Decorrelation for Query Q1

Clearly, the main advantage of this approach is that the independent expression is evaluated only once. In addition, if the Semi-Join's implementation uses a custom data structure (e.g. a hash-table) to improve performance, this data structure has to be initialized only once, compared to one initialization per student in the naïve correlated evaluation from Fig. 1. However, decorrelation comes at a price: The outer expression produces duplicates which have to be eliminated. Below, we show how we can avoid them using the novel Kappa-Join. Our evaluation in Sec. 5 confirms this claim.

3.3   Kappa-Join

To avoid the above-mentioned generation of duplicates, but nevertheless gain performance by avoiding unneeded evaluations of the independent expression, we introduce the Kappa-Join operator. It combines the advantages of the evaluation strategies from Fig. 2 and Fig. 1 into one operator and capitalizes on efficient implementation techniques.

Logical Definition. The *Kappa-Join* is a ternary operator, i.e. it has three argument expressions e_1, e_2, and e_3. It is defined by the equation

$$e_1 \kappa^{e_2}_{cn=cn'} e_3 := \sigma_{\exists_{x;\,exists}(e_2 \ltimes_{cn=cn'} e_3)}(e_1)$$

where cn is the context node resulting from the evaluation of e_2 and cn' the context node from e_3. As for conventional join operators, we denote the producer expressions

---

[1] In [23] this operator is called MapConcat.

e_1 and e_3 the as *outer producer* and *inner producer*, respectively. The second producer expression e_2 (in the superscript) is called *link producer* because it acts as a link between the outer and inner producer within the join predicate. The outer expression e_1 and the inner expression e_3 are independent expressions, i.e. they do not depend on any of the Kappa-Join's other arguments. In contrast, the expression e_2 is dependent on e_1.

Informally, the result sequence of the operator contains all tuples from the outer producer (e_1) for which there exists at least one tuple in the link producer (e_2), when evaluated with respect to the current tuple of e_1, that satisfies the predicate p which is a comparison from attributes of e_2 and attributes of the the inner producer (e_3).

Translation with Kappa-Join. There exist two alternatives to incorporate the Kappa-Join into an algebraic plan: (1) The Kappa-Join's definition matches the pattern that results from the canonical translation of correlation predicates (e.g. see Fig. 1). Hence, the Kappa-Join can *replace* this pattern after translation and, hence, already decorrelate during translation. (2) The other alternative is to *modify* the translation procedure such that a Kappa-Join is used for conjunctive correlation predicates.

Because our experiments (see Sec. 5) show that the Kappa-Join always dominates the canonical approach and simplifies the translation procedure, we have chosen the second alternative. Fig. 3 contains the resulting algebra expression for Q1. Here, the location path `//student` is mapped to the outer producer of the

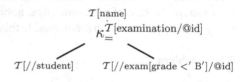

Fig. 3. Query Q1 with Kappa-Join

Kappa-Join . The inner location path `examination/@id` is the (dependent) link producer, and the independent expression `//exam[grade<'B']/@id` is mapped to the inner producer.

OPEN
```
1   while T ← INNERPRODUCER.NEXT
2       do HASHTABLE.INSERT (T)
```

NEXT
```
1    while T₁ ← OUTERPRODUCER.NEXT
2        do
3            LINKPRODUCER.OPEN(T₁)
4            while T₂ ← LINKPRODUCER.NEXT
5                do
6                    if HASHTABLE.LOOKUP(T₂)
7                        then
8                            LINKPRODUCER.CLOSE
9                            return T₁
10
11           LINKPRODUCER.CLOSE
12   return nil
```

Fig. 4. Pseudocode for the Kappa-Join

Implementation. The secret of the Kappa-Join lies in its simple, yet efficient implementation. It improves performance beyond that of the operator combination in its logical definition. Fig. 4 shows the pseudocode for the implementation of the Kappa-Join as an iterator [14].

In its open method, the Kappa-Join builds a data structure, e.g. a hash-table, containing the attributes from the inner producer that are part of the join predicate. In its next method, the Kappa-Join initializes the link producer for every tuple T_1 from its outer producer. Like a Semi-Join, it then probes the hash-table with tuples T_2 from the link producer until a matching one is found, and returns the outer tuple as soon as it finds a match. The Kappa-Join does not always enumerate all tuples from the dependent link producer, while building the hash-table once only. Hence, the worst-case complexity is $O(|e_1| \times |e_2| + |e_3|)$, assuming constant hash-table insert and lookup, respectively. However, the average complexity depends on the distribution of the data and is usually much better. Compared to the algebra plan from Fig. 2, the plan in Fig. 3 using the Kappa-Join has three main advantages: (1) it avoids to enumerate all tuples from the link producer because it immediately returns a result if one match is found (see Line 9). (2) It does not produce duplicates of tuples from the outer producer because the result contains at most one tuple from $T[//\text{student}]$, and (3) consequently saves the cost of a final duplicate elimination. These effects combine to yield the speedup that can be achieved (see Sec. 5).

4 Kappa-Join for Disjunctive Correlation

In the previous section, we demonstrated how complex correlation predicates that occur in a conjunction can be evaluated efficiently. However, as shown in our Example Q2, correlation predicates can also occur disjunctively. Several optimization techniques for queries containing non-correlated disjunctive predicates have been proposed [7,8,16]. One of them is the Bypass technique [8], that is used to avoid unnecessary evaluations. However, to the best of our knowledge, nobody has shown how to decorrelate disjunctively occurring correlation predicates. In this section, we show how this can be achieved.

4.1 Problem

Consider the canonical algebra plan for Query Q2 (see Fig. 5). This algebra expression is similar to the one presented in Fig. 1 for Q1, except for the *or* function call in the subscript of the Selection. Disjunctively occurring literals are translated using an *or* function call. It evaluates to true if either of its producer expressions does.

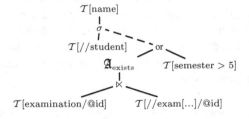

Fig. 5. Translation sketch for Q2

The pattern used for the correlation predicate does not match the definition of the Kappa-Join because of the extra literal. Hence, we cannot proceed as for Query Q1. The only technique currently available to improve the canonical plan is the so-called shortcut evaluation of the disjunction, which means that we can avoid evaluation of the expensive correlation predicate for those students where the cheaper literal semester > 5 is true. Below, we recall the Bypass technique which does exactly that.

4.2 Bypass Technique

The Bypass technique was used to prevent the unnecessary evaluation of predicates that occur disjunctively [8]. For this, the Bypass technique adds a new class of operators to the conventional algebra. In contrast to regular operators, Bypass operators have *two* output sequences. The first sequence contains the tuples that qualify for the operator's predicate. The second sequence consists of all other tuples. The two disjoint sequences are called *true-* and *false-sequence*. The existing Bypass technique provides a Bypass

Selection, a Bypass Join and a Bypass Semi-Join [8]. For the purpose of this paper, we only need the Bypass Selection.

Consider as a first example the algebra representation of Q2 extended by a Bypass Selection operator $(\sigma^{\pm})$ for evaluating the cheaper predicate semester > 5. Fig. 6 shows the resulting plan. Here and in the following, the false-sequence is indicated by dotted lines. The evaluation according to this plan starts with computing all result tuples for the outer expression $(//\text{student})$.

The Bypass Selection divides these tuples into two disjoint sequences. The true-sequence contains the students that fulfill the predicate semester > 5. Accordingly, the false-sequence contains the tuples that fail this predicate. The tuples of both sequences form two separate paths which are merged by $\dot{\cup}$. The tuples from the false-sequence

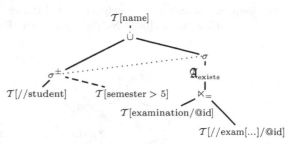

Fig. 6. Q2 with Bypass Selection

must pass the second Selection operator computing the complex correlation predicate. This operator is responsible for filtering out those tuples that do not qualify for any of the two predicates. The two sequences are disjoint. Hence, no duplicate elimination is required by $\dot{\cup}$. However, as the XPath semantics requires its result to be in document order, a merge as in merge-sort may be required. This can be done, for example, by numbering the tuples or use node ids if they represent order. The final processing of $\mathcal{T}[\text{name}]$ completes the result.

Looking at Fig. 6, we are in for a surprise: The Bypass Selection we introduced to allow shortcut evaluation of the disjunction made the Kappa-Join pattern reappear! We discuss in the following subsection how to leverage this for decorrelation of disjunctive queries with a single correlation predicate.

4.3 Kappa-Join for a Single Disjunctive Correlation Predicate

Query Q2 contains a single correlation predicate within a disjunction. Bypass plans have the advantage that the expression in the false-sequence can be optimized separately. In general, whenever there is only a single correlation predicate per disjunction we can apply decorrelation. As seen in

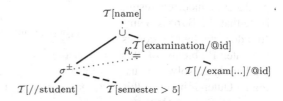

Fig. 7. Q2 with Bypass Selection and Kappa-Join

Fig. 6, we can again recognize the pattern that allows us to integrate the Kappa-Join for the conjunctive case. In the false-sequence of Fig. 6, we can use the Kappa-Join, yielding the expression shown in Fig. 7.

In this case, the plan takes advantage of both: (1) shortcut evaluation of the literals connected by disjunction, and (2) decorrelation of correlation predicates allowing efficient execution if the cheaper predicate in the disjunction fails.

4.4   Kappa-Join for Multiple Disjunctive Correlation Predicates

We have seen that the Bypass technique facilitates decorrelation if there is only one correlation predicate in the disjunction. Unfortunately, if there is more than one, we are again at a loss. Consider as an example the following Query Q3. In addition to the good students, we also want to query the database for students that have already been a teaching assistant for a given lecture.

//student[examination/@id= //exam[grade < 'B']/@id or   **Q3**
        @id = //lecture[title='NCT']/helpers/helper/@student]/name

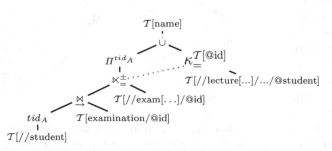

Fig. 8. Incorrect decorrelated bypass plan for Q3

We would like to decorrelate both correlation predicates. At first glance, it is tempting to apply the decorrelation strategy that was discussed in Sec. 3.2. Fig. 8 shows an algebra expression for Q3 applying this technique, but using a Bypass Semi-Join instead of a regular Semi-Join. However, this approach is not feasible. The first D-Join on the leftmost branch of the plan eliminates those items produced by //student for which the dependent expression exmination/@id produces an empty result. If we have a conjunctive query, this is no problem.

However, the //student items failing the first disjunct could still qualify for the second disjunct, and dropping them as in Fig. 8 produces an incorrect result. Note that the Bypass Semi-Join does not help: it comes too late. Problems of this kind are often solved by using an Outer-Join, or in this case outer D-Join. However,

$$\mathcal{T}[name]$$
$$\kappa_{=}^{\mathcal{T}}[@id]$$
$$\mathcal{T}[//lecture[...]/.../@student]$$
$$\kappa_{=}^{\pm,\mathcal{T}}[examination/@id]$$
$$\mathcal{T}[//student] \quad \mathcal{T}[//exam[...]/@id]$$

Fig. 9. Bypass plan sketches for Q2 with Kappa-Join

this would still require duplicate elimination on tid_A, as shown in the true-sequence.

It turns out that we can do much better by applying the *Bypass Kappa-Join*. As every bypass operator, the Bypass Kappa-Join has two result sequences. The true-sequence is the same as for the regular Kappa-Join. The tuples in the false-sequence are the ones from the outer producer for which there was no match in the inner producer or for which the link producer returned an empty result. In the false-stream, we now have our familiar pattern and can employ the decorrelation strategy as if the correlation predicate was a single correlation predicate. Fig. 9 shows the result. This plan finally has everything we want: (1) the evaluation of both correlation predicates can be done in a decorrelated fashion, (2) the Kappa-Join avoids unneeded duplicate generation and elimination for both correlation predicates, and (3) we have shortcut evaluation and evaluate the second correlation predicate only if the first fails.

5   Evaluation

To show the effectiveness of our approach, we ran experiments with different XPath evaluation engines against our canonical and optimized approaches. Additionally, we performed measurements that compare the existing decorrelation strategy against the new Kappa-Join operator. We chose the freely available engines

- Xalan C++ 1.8.0 using Xerces C++ version 2.6.0,
- Saxon for Java 8.7.1,
- Berkeley DB XML 2.0.9 (DBXML) using libpathan 1.99 as XPath engine,
- MonetDB 4.8.0 using MonetDB-XQuery-0.8.0,
- the evaluator provided by the XMLTaskForce [19] (XTF), and
- Natix [10] for the execution of the canonical, decorrelated (ICDE06 [5]), and Kappa-Join plans.

5.1   Environment

The environment we used to perform the experiments consisted of a PC with an Intel Pentium 4 CPU at 2.40GHz and 1 GB of RAM, running Linux 2.6.11-smp. The Natix C++ library was compiled with gcc 3.3.5 with optimization level 2.

For Xalan, Saxon, and XTF, we measured the net time to *execute* the query. The time needed to parse the document and generate the main memory representation is subtracted from the elapsed evaluation time. For the evaluation of MonetDB, Berkeley DB XML and Natix, we imported the documents into the database. The time needed for this is not included in the execution times. The queries were executed several times with an empty buffer pool and without any indexes.

Documents. We generated two different sets of documents. The first set is used for the example queries Q1-Q3 used throughout this paper. These documents were generated by the ToXgene data generator [1]^2. The smallest document contains 50 employees, 100 students, 10 lectures and 30 exams. With each document we quadrupled these numbers. That is, the biggest document contains 51200 employees, 102400 students, 10240 lectures and 30720 exams. This led to moderate document sizes between 59kB and 43MB.

The second set is used for the comparison of the existing decorrelation strategy and the new Kappa-Join operator. We generated seven documents structured according to the following template:

---

^{2} The DTD as well as the generator template file are listed in the appendix of our technical report [21].

```
<?xml version='1.0'?>
<gen>
<e1 id='0'> <e2 id='0'/> ... i-e2 nodes <e2 id='i'/> </e1>
                          ...
<e1 id='0'> <e2 id='0'/> ... i-e2 nodes <e2 id='i'/> </e1>
<e3 id='RandomNumber'/>
</gen>
```

Each of the documents contains 1000 e1 nodes and 1000 e3 nodes. For each document we varied the number of e2 nodes (under an e1 node) between 10 and 500 nodes. This gave us documents between 252kB and 13M.

Queries. We executed performance measurements for all example queries (Q1, Q2, and Q3) presented throughout this paper. For Natix, we generated several different query evaluation plans. For each of the queries we generated the canonical plan as specified in [4]. For example, Fig. 1 shows the plans for Q1. Further, we generated plans incorporating our optimization strategies. Fig. 10 maps names for optimized query evaluation plans to figures that illustrate the used techniques.

Query	Name	Figure
Q1	decorr	Fig. 2
	kappa	Fig. 3
Q2	bypass	Fig. 6
	kappa	Fig. 7
Q3	bypasskappa	Fig. 9

Fig. 10. Query Evaluation Plans

Additionally, we executed performance measurements that compare the existing decorrelation strategy with our Kappa-Join operator. Therefore, we executed the following query on the synthetic data set:

/gen/e1[e2/@id = /gen/e3/@id]   **Q4**

5.2   Results and Interpretation

Fig. 11 contains the results of our performance measurements (elapsed time in seconds). The best execution time(s) for each column in all tables are printed in bold face. Those that did not finish within 6 hours are marked by DNF (did not finish). For MonetDB the evaluation of some queries ran out of memory on bigger documents. These cases are denoted by OOM.

Subfigures 11(a), 11(b), and 11(c) show the execution times for Q1, Q2, and Q3, respectively. For all queries on all documents, our decorrelated approach performs and scales best. Especially for the disjunctive queries Q2 and Q3, the performance of all other approaches drops considerably when executed on bigger documents. In contrast, our plans containing the Kappa-Join (Q2) and Bypass Kappa-Join (Q3) almost scale linearly with the size of the document.

For Q1 the execution times of the existing decorrelation approach (called ICDE06 [5]) behave similar to those of the Kappa-Join. This is because all students took very few exams, i.e. only between one and three. For this reason, we compared those two strategies on the synthetic data set. Subfigure 11(d) compares the two strategies. The execution

Evaluator	Documents					
	1	2	3	4	5	6
Xalan	0.30	0.38	6.17	95.6	1552	DNF
DBXML	0.07	0.66	11.6	336	DNF	DNF
MonetDB	0.31	0.38	2.05	36.1	OOM	OOM
Saxon	0.21	0.28	0.53	1.49	11.14	141
XTF	0.40	4.72	82.8	DNF	DNF	DNF
Natix						
•canonical	0.25	2.62	38.2	583	9637	DNF
•decorr	**0.02**	**0.03**	**0.06**	**0.19**	**0.75**	2.99
•kappa	**0.02**	**0.03**	**0.06**	**0.19**	**0.75**	**2.88**

(a) Query Q1

Evaluator	Documents					
	1	2	3	4	5	6
Xalan	**0.02**	0.23	3.63	54.7	893	12453
DBXML	0.06	0.39	6.87	207	DNF	DNF
MonetDB	0.25	0.36	2.02	36.2	OOM	OOM
Saxon	0.22	0.30	0.62	1.44	7.82	85.4
XTF	0.76	8.60	9180	DNF	DNF	DNF
Natix						
•canonical	0.16	1.64	20.9	333	5598	DNF
•bypass	0.16	1.59	20.7	323	5436	DNF
•kappa	0.03	**0.05**	**0.16**	**0.60**	**2.51**	**9.91**

(b) Query Q2

Evaluator	Documents					
	1	2	3	4	5	6
Xalan	0.06	0.75	12.6	199	3201	DNF
DBXML	0.30	1.61	30.2	4057	DNF	DNF
MonetDB	0.31	0.50	3.29	62.9	OOM	OOM
Saxon	0.20	0.28	0.54	1.48	10.9	138
XTF	0.48	5.14	94.8	DNF	DNF	DNF
Natix						
•canonical	0.37	3.49	DNF	DNF	DNF	DNF
•bypasscanonical	0.37	3.43	48.1	749	12492	DNF
•bypasskappa	**0.02**	**0.04**	**0.10**	**0.35**	**1.44**	**5.91**

(c) Query Q3

(d) ICDE06 vs. Kappa-Join (Q4)

Fig. 11. Performance measurements

times of the existing decorrelation strategy grow linearly with the number of e2 nodes per e1 node. This is because it has to enumerate all e2 nodes and finally perform a duplicate elimination on the appropriate e1 nodes. The execution times of the Kappa-Join operator are almost constant because the Kappa-Join does not need to enumerate all e2 nodes and saves the cost of a final duplicate elimination.

6   Related Work

Work on XPath evaluation falls into three general categories. In the first category, we have main memory interpreters like Xalan, XSLTProc, and [13]. Clearly, these approaches do not scale well. In the second category, we find work where XML is shredded into relational systems and XPath is evaluated on this shredded representation. In this category we find approaches like Pathfinder [3]. The problem with this approach are the numerous joins that have to be executed. Finally, the third category uses a native (tree) algebraic approach. Here, we find SAL [2], TAX [15], yet another algebra [25], and [4]. None of the approaches in any of three classes performs decorrelation.

In the relational and object-oriented context, decorrelation has been studied extensively [9,11,12,17,18,26]. Similar techniques have been proposed for the evaluation of XQuery and XPath [5,20]. Gottlob et.al [13] also proposed an approach that avoids multiple evaluations of XPath expressions.

Several optimization techniques for queries containing disjunctive predicates have been proposed [7,8,16]. One of them is the Bypass technique [8], which we extend with support for decorrelation. Because bypass operators have two output streams, which are unioned later, the resulting expression forms a directed acyclic graph (DAG). Strategies for implementing Bypass operators and query evaluation engines that support DAG-structured query plans can be found in [8,22,24]. In [6] we extend our technique for decorrelating SQL queries with disjunctive predicates.

7 Conclusion

We demonstrate how to efficiently evaluate XML queries featuring existentially quantified correlation predicates. To this end, we have introduced the novel Kappa-Join operator that naturally fits into algebraic execution plans for quantified correlation predicates. It is simple to implement and yet highly efficient. However, if disjunctions come into play, the Kappa-Join and *all* known decorrelation techniques fail. By injecting the Kappa-Join with the Bypass technique, we are also able to perform decorrelated evaluation if the correlation predicate occurs in a disjunction. All other approaches cannot evaluate such a case efficiently. Our performance measurements show that the Kappa-Join outperforms existing approaches by up to two orders of magnitude.

Encouraged by these results, we plan to enhance our approach by incorporating further optimization techniques into it. These include handling of magic sets (to optimize dependent expressions) and factorizing common subexpressions. However, our future work does not stop here. We also want to introduce cost functions for our algebraic operators (especially the Kappa-Join) to enable an optimizer to choose between different evaluation plans.

Acknowledgments. We would like to thank Simone Seeger for her comments on the manuscript.

References

1. D. Barbosa, A. Mendelzon, J. Keenleyside, and K. Lyons. ToXgene: a template-based data generator for XML. In *Proceedings of the ACM Sigmod, Madison, USA*, 2002.
2. C. Beeri and Y. Tzaban. SAL: An algebra for semistructured data and XML. In *WebDB (Informal Proceedings)*, pages 37–42, 1999.
3. P. A. Boncz, T. Grust, S. Manegold, J. Rittinger, and J. Teubner. Pathfinder: Relational xquery over multi-gigabyte XML inputs in interactive time. Technical Report INS-E0503, CWI, March 2005. MonetDB 4.8.0, Pathfinder 0.8.0.
4. M. Brantner, S. Helmer, C-C. Kanne, and G. Moerkotte. Full-fledged Algebraic XPath Processing in Natix. In *Proceedings of the ICDE Conference, Tokyo, Japan*, pages 705–716, 2005.
5. M. Brantner, C-C. Kanne, S. Helmer, and G. Moerkotte. Algebraic Optimization of Nested XPath Expressions. In *Proceedings of the ICDE Conference, Atlanta*, page 128, 2006.
6. M. Brantner, N. May, and G. Moerkotte. Unnesting SQL queries in the presence of disjunction. Technical report, University of Mannheim, March 2006. http://db.informatik.uni-mannheim.de/publications/TR-06-001.pdf.
7. F. Bry. Towards an efficient evaluation of general queries: quantifier and disjunction processing revisited. In *Proceedings of ACM SIGMOD Conference, Oregon, USA*, pages 193–204, 1989.

8. J. Claußen, A. Kemper, G. Moerkotte, K. Peithner, and M. Steinbrunn. Optimization and evaluation of disjunctive queries. *IEEE Trans. Knowl. Data Eng.*, 12(2):238–260, 2000.
9. U. Dayal. Of nests and trees: A unified approach to processing queries that contain nested subqueries, aggregates, and quantifiers. In *Proceedings of the VLDB Conference, Brighton, England*, pages 197–208, 1987.
10. T. Fiebig, S. Helmer, C-C. Kanne, G. Moerkotte, J. Neumann, R. Schiele, and T. Westmann. Anatomy of a native XML base management system. *VLDB Journal*, 11(4):292–314, 2002.
11. C. Galindo-Legaria and M. Joshi. Orthogonal optimization of subqueries and aggregation. In *Proceedings of ACM SIGMOD Conference, Santa Barbara, USA*, pages 571–581, 2001.
12. R. A. Ganski and H. K. T. Wong. Optimization of nested sql queries revisited. In *Proceedings of the ACM SIGMOD, San Francisco, California*, pages 23–33. ACM Press, 1987.
13. G. Gottlob, C. Koch, and R. Pichler. XPath query evaluation: Improving time and space efficiency. In *Proceedings of the ICDE Conference, Bangalore, India*, pages 379–390, 2003.
14. Goetz Graefe. Query evaluation techniques for large databases. *ACM Computing Surveys*, 25(2):73–170, 1993.
15. H. V. Jagadish, L. V. S. Lakshmanan, D. Srivastava, and K. Thompson. Tax: A tree algebra for xml. In *Prcoceedings of the DBPL Conference, Frascati, Italy*, pages 149–164, 2001.
16. M. Jarke and J. Koch. Query optimization in database systems. *ACM Computing Surveys*, 16(2):111–152, June 1984.
17. W. Kiessling. SQL-like and Quel-like correlation queries with aggregates revisited. ERL/UCB Memo 84/75, University of Berkeley, 1984.
18. W. Kim. On optimizing an SQL-like nested query. *j-TODS*, 7(3):443–469, September 1982.
19. C. Koch. XMLTaskForce XPath evaluator, 2004. Released 2004-09-30.
20. N. May, S. Helmer, and G. Moerkotte. Nested queries and quantifiers in an ordered context. In *Proceedings of the ICDE Conference, Boston, MA, USA*, pages 239–250, 2004.
21. M.Brantner, S.Helmer, C-C. Kanne, and G. Moerkotte.   Kappa-Join: Efficient Execution of Existential Quantification in XML Query Languages.   Technical Report TR-2006-001, University of Mannheim, 2006.   http://pi3.informatik.uni-mannheim.de/publikationenDetails.html.en#ID514.
22. T. Neumann. *Efficient Generation and Execution of DAG-Structured Query Graphs*. PhD thesis, University of Mannheim, 2005.
23. C. Re, J. Siméon, and M. F. Fernández. A complete and efficient algebraic compiler for xquery. In *Proceedings of the ICDE Conference, Atlanta, USA*, page 14, 2006.
24. P. Roy. Optimization of DAG-structured query evaluation plans. Master's thesis, Indian Institute of Technology, Bombay, 1998.
25. C. Sartiani and A. Albano. Yet another query algebra for xml data. In *Proceedings of the IDEAS Conference, Edmonton, Canada*, pages 106–115, 2002.
26. P. Seshadri, H. Pirahesh, and T. Y. Cliff Leung. Complex query decorrelation. In *Proceedings of the ICDE Conference, New Orleans, USA*, pages 450–458, 1996.

Index vs. Navigation in XPath Evaluation

Norman May, Matthias Brantner, Alexander Böhm,
Carl-Christian Kanne, and Guido Moerkotte

University of Mannheim
68131 Mannheim, Germany
{norman, msb, boehm, cc, moer}@db.informatik.uni-mannheim.de

Abstract. A well-known rule of thumb claims, it is better to scan than to use an index when more than 10% of the data are accessed. This rule was formulated for relational databases. But is it still valid for XML queries? In this paper we develop similar rules of thumb for XML queries by experimentally comparing different execution strategies, e.g. using navigation or indices. These rules can be used immediately for heuristic optimization of XML queries, and in the long run, they may serve as a foundation for cost-based query optimization in XQuery.

1 Motivation

XPath is used as a stand-alone query language and as part of XSLT or XQuery to address parts of an XML document. As an increasing number of applications rely on one of these query languages, efficient evaluation of XPath expressions has emerged as a focal point of research. In particular, efficient retrieval techniques must be chosen when queries access large instances of XML documents. Three core aspects influence their performance:

1. storage structures [2,11,12,16,8,21,28,7],
2. algorithms to evaluate XPath queries [1,15,16,10,27,6], and
3. an optimizer that selects a cost-optimal retrieval method given 1 and 2.

As the (incomplete) list of citations indicates, many proposals exist for the first two aspects. However, research on optimization of XPath has just scratched the surface. The only cost-based optimizers we know [5,29] are limited to index-based storage structures for which estimating access costs does not fundamentally differ from relational storage. Most query engines only perform heuristic optimizations. Instead, we expect to find better query execution plans when cost-based optimization is used. Nevertheless, it would already help if we had simple rules of thumb, as established for relational databases [14]. In particular, is it still true for XML queries that it is better to scan (or navigate) than to use an index when more than 10% of the data are accessed?

In this paper we analyze the performance of known techniques for the evaluation of structural XPath queries. Particularly, we use Natix [11] to compare the following two execution strategies: (1) navigation through the logical structure of

S. Amer-Yahia et al. (Eds.): XSym 2006, LNCS 4156, pp. 16–30, 2006.

the document and (2) index-based retrieval in conjunction with structural joins. Our findings can be applied to improve heuristics used in XPath query optimizers. In the long term, such experiments will help us to derive cost information which can be used by cost-based XQuery optimizers.

To be able to derive costs, it is important to understand the architecture that underlies query evaluation. Hence, we present an abstract model for storing XML documents in Sec. 2. This storage model includes indices which employ XML node labeling schemes. In Sec. 3 we proceed with an overview of NAL, the Natix physical algebra. The algebraic operators included in NAL form the building blocks for the query evaluation plans we investigate in Sec. 4. These evaluation plans are experimentally compared in Sec. 5. Our experiments show that there is not only one best choice for evaluating XPath expressions. But it is still true that index based-techniques are often superior when only small parts of the data are touched by a query. In contrast, full scans perform better when large fragments of the input qualify for the query result. Based on these results, we conclude the paper and discuss future work (Sec. 6).

2   The Storage Model

Since retrieving data is one of the main cost drivers for XML query evaluation, it is important to understand how XML data is stored and how it can be accessed. In this section we briefly survey fundamental techniques available to access XML data.

2.1   Physical XML Storage

The most general approach to store XML data maps the logical structure of an XML document to physical storage structures. These physical storage structures offer primitives to directly navigate through the logical structure of the XML document. Consequently, it is possible to reconstruct the logical structure of the original document from its physical representation. While there are many possible implementations for this mapping, e.g. [4,11,16,8,7,27,28], we believe that some general ideas are shared by all storage schemes:

1. Fragments of the XML document are assigned to storage units.
2. The document structure can be reconstructed from the physical storage.
3. The cost to access a part of the document depends on its storage location.

Consider the XML document depicted in Fig. 1 as an ordered labeled tree. The nodes in the tree correspond to element nodes, and the edges represent parent-child relationships. A main memory representation, e.g. DOM, assigns an address in main memory to each node in the tree. Pointers connect a node to its children, siblings, or parent. It is quite easy to see that the logical document structure can be reconstructed from this representation by traversing the pointers. Given the node with subscript 1.1.1.1, one can imagine that accessing its first child might be cheaper than accessing a node that is further away in the document

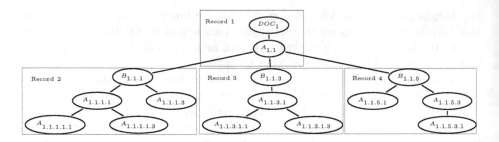

Fig. 1. The tree representation of an XML document

structure, e.g. the node with subscript 1.1.5.3. The latter operation might even require disk I/O if the target node does not reside in physical main memory.

Natix assigns fragments of XML documents to records of variable size and stores them on physical pages on disk [11]. The logical structure of the document is preserved by a structured storage inside the records and by references to other records. A physical storage address (NID) is assigned to each node. It is used to implement these references or to directly access XML nodes. The document in Fig. 1, for instance, is mapped to four physical records. It is possible to traverse nodes inside a record or to navigate to other records in the XML store. Navigation to a record on another page results in disk I/O if this page is not yet in the main memory buffer. The cost of this page access depends on the characteristics of the storage device and the location of the page on disk.

2.2   XML Node Labels

For efficient XML query evaluation, we want to support indices. Additionally, we require an efficient processing of updates. Hence, we employ logical node identifiers (LIDs) to abstract from physical storage locations. In Natix we have implemented LIDs as ORDPATH IDs [9]. As an incarnation of Dewey IDs [3], they satisfy the two requirements mentioned above. Furthermore, ORDPATH IDs support efficient query processing because given two LIDs, it is possible to test their structural relationship with respect to any XPath axis. In the document shown in Fig. 1, the subscript of each node represents the ORDPATH ID assigned to this node.

2.3   Indexing XML

We index XML documents in B^+-trees as proposed by Chien at. al [2]. There exist many other proposals for indexing XML documents, e.g. [12,21]. But we believe that our approach provides a solid performance for a wide range of queries and at the same time supports efficient concurrent updates.

The index we use in Natix is an implementation of a B^+-tree with sibling links based on the algorithms proposed by Jaluta et. al [20]. This B-link index allows storing keys of variable size and performs online rebalancing and deallocation operations in case of underutilized nodes. These operations are especially

beneficial as the index performance does not deteriorate due to document updates, and explicit garbage collection operations become obsolete. Other specific
features useful for processing ORDPATH IDs include key-range scans exploiting
the sibling links and high concurrency by restricting the number of latches to a
minimum.

The general idea of our indexing scheme
is shown in Fig. 2. We create two indices:
one called *Tag2Lid* and the other *Lid2Nid*.

Tag2Lid maps tag names to LIDs. The key
value is the tag name, and the indexed
value is the LID. For the same tag name,
LIDs are returned in document order,
i.e. in ascending order.

Lid2Nid maps LIDs to their physical storage address. This index is optional when
the storage manager directly provides
access to XML fragments based on their
LID. However, for generality we will ex-
plicitly use this index to locate result
nodes of an XPath expression.

Tag2Lid		Lid2Nid	
Tag	Lid	Lid	Nid
A	1.1	1	1
A	1.1.1.1	1.1	2
A	1.1.1.1.1	1.1.1	3
...	...	1.1.1.1	4
A	1.1.5.3	...	
A	1.1.5.3.1	1.1.5	12
B	1.1.1	1.1.5.1	13
B	1.1.3	1.1.5.3	14
B	1.1.5	1.1.5.3.1	15
DOC	1		

Fig. 2. Indexing XML documents

3   Execution Model

Besides the physical storage structures, the cost of a query execution plan is
determined by the algorithms it uses to access the data and to evaluate the
query. Hence, we also need to comment on the available algorithms. We present
an algebraic approach to XPath evaluation because both an algebraic query
optimizer and an evaluation engine is easy to extend with new operators [1,27].
Additionally, we want to benefit from the experiences gathered with cost-based
algebraic optimizers built for relational and object-oriented databases. The Natix
Physical Algebra includes all algebraic operators we need to implement the query
execution plans (QEPs) discussed in Sec. 4.

3.1   Architecture and Notation

Our physical algebra works on sequences of tuples. Each tuple contains a set of
variable bindings representing the attributes of the tuple. Some physical operators extend these bindings by appending attribute-value pairs to a tuple. All
operators are implemented as conventional iterators [13]. Tuples are passed in
a pipelined fashion from the argument operator to its consumer. The set of
supported operators we cover here comprises the common algorithms used to
execute XPath queries [1,10,27].

To test structural relationships between LIDs or XML nodes, we arrange for
the following notations: We denote with $n \Downarrow m$ that m is descendent of n and
with $n \downarrow m$ that m is child of n.

3.2   General Operators

The following operators are used independently of the XPath evaluation method. The *Singleton Scan* ($\square$) returns a singleton sequence consisting of the empty tuple. We denote the *Map* operator by $\chi_{a:e_2}(e_1)$. It extends each tuple t in e_1 with attribute a. The value bound to a is computed by evaluating the subscript e_2 with variable bindings taken from t. For example, we use the Map operator to dereference physical node ids, i.e. $\chi_{n:*a}(e_1)$, or to retrieve the root node of a document, i.e. $\chi_{r:root}(e_1)$. To remove duplicates on a set of attributes A, we use a *Duplicate Elimination* operator ($\Pi_A^D(e)$). To rename a set of attributes A into another set of attributes A', we use $\Pi_{A':A}(e)$. Some evaluation strategies require us to reestablish document order on a sequence of nodes bound to attribute a. Therefore, we employ the sort operator ($Sort_a$). The *D-Join*, denoted by $e_1 \underset{\rightarrow}{\bowtie} e_2$, joins each tuple t in e_1 with all tuples returned by the evaluation of e_2. The result returned by e_2 depends on the attribute bindings of t. Similar to the MapConcat operator in [27], it is used to concatenate the evaluation of location steps inside a location path.

3.3   XPath Navigation Operators

In this paper we use the *Unnest-Map* operator $\Upsilon_{cn:c/a::n}(e)$ to evaluate XPath location steps by navigation. Given a context node stored in variable c of a tuple $t \in e$, it evaluates axis a and applies node test n to the remaining candidate nodes. Each result node is bound to variable cn in the result tuple. During the evaluation of a location step the operator navigates through the document that potentially contains result nodes. This traversal is done for every context node.

3.4   Index-Aware Operators

For efficient XPath evaluation the *Structural Join* ($e_1 \bowtie_p^{ST-J} e_2$) was proposed [6]. It joins one sequence of tuples of context nodes, e_1, with a sequence of candidate nodes, e_2. Both sequences are sorted in document order. Predicate p tests the axis step relation that must hold between nodes of the two sequences. We classify the Structural Join as index-aware because it solely uses information provided by the LIDs and thus only relies on index information.

We employ the *IndexScan* ($Idx_{n;A;p;rp}$) to access data stored in a B-link tree named n, e.g. the index "Tag2Lid" or "Lid2Nid". A is a set of attribute bindings established by the scan. It must be a subset of the attributes defined in the schema of the index. Predicate p optionally tests the upper and lower bound. Residual predicate rp is an optional predicate applied to each tuple before it is passed to the consumer operator.

4   Query Execution Plans

In Sections 2 and 3 we have laid the foundation for several evaluation techniques available for XPath. We now discuss the following types of query execution plans (QEPs):

1. Navigate through the XML document (e.g. in a DOM-like fashion) [1].
2. Use indices to access the candidate nodes of each navigation step and relate them by join operations to evaluate the query. If there are multiple navigation steps, we have two more choices:
   (a) Access indices in the order specified in the query.
   (b) Reorder the index accesses and possibly sort the result nodes at the end [29].

In our opinion, these types of QEPs comprise a wide variety of XPath evaluation techniques that have not been compared yet. For each alternative mentioned above, we present a QEP for the query /DOC/TAG1/TAG2. Even this simple query allows us to point out the advantages of each alternative. The reason is that each QEP exploits structural relationships, selectivities of location steps, or physical storage characteristics to different degrees. As we will see in our experiments, there is no single plan that is consistently faster than the other alternatives.

4.1   Plan Using Navigation

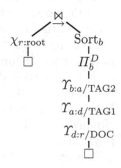

The most direct translation of the XPath expression results in a navigational plan [1]. The result of the *stacked translation* of the query into our algebra is depicted in Fig. 3. The topmost operator of the QEP is a D-Join which initializes the context for the XPath query evaluation to the root node. The right argument is evaluated with the bindings taken from this context. The stacked translation results in a sequence of Unnest-Map operators, each of which evaluates one location step. In general, to compute the resulting node set, duplicates have to be removed, and the result nodes have to be sorted by document order. In our example query duplicate elimination or sorting can be avoided [17,18].

Fig. 3. Plan using navigation

When the QEP is evaluated, each Unnest-Map operator traverses some part of the document, starting at the current context node. E.g. during a child step all children of the current context node will be visited. When a node satisfies all node tests, it is passed to the next operator where it may serve as another context node.

This evaluation strategy has three basic consequences: (1) Non-matching nodes may implicitly prune parts of the document from the traversal. Thereby, accessing physical pages is avoided for potentially large parts of the document. (2) Location steps may visit intermediate nodes that will never be part of a matching location path. E.g. for descendant steps we have to look at all descendant nodes of the context node. (3) During the document traversal, visiting physical pages may lead to random I/O and multiple visits to the same physical page.

4.2   Plan Using Index

The motivation for using an index is to retrieve only nodes with tag names that satisfy a query predicate. The translation into a plan using an index is an

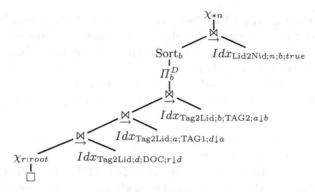

Fig. 4. Plan with index access in order

application of the *canonical translation* presented in [1] or the XQuery translation of [10].

The result of this translation is shown in Fig. 4. The data flow of the QEP goes from the bottom-left leaf node upwards to the root of the QEP. First, the root node is initialized as context node. This context can be used to restrict the range scan in the index "Tag2Lid". This index access is performed in the dependent part of each D-Join in the plan. We have to apply the residual predicate to each node retrieved from the index. Together with the range predicate, this test completes the structural test between context node and document node. Before all physical nodes are retrieved, we possibly have to perform a duplicate elimination and a sort [18]. Finally, we employ the index "Lid2Nid" to get the physical nodes of the query result and access the physical nodes on disk using a Map operator. Note that some queries do not require this final dereferencing step, e.g. quantified queries or queries with count aggregate. This can be used in favour of such queries.

The index-based technique has the following properties: (1) It only considers nodes which can match the node tests in the query. (2) The index is repeatedly accessed for each context node. This results in random I/O, as the same index is accessed for different location steps. (3) Context information can be used to prune the set of candidate nodes. This depends on the availability of e.g. level information for axis steps to sibling nodes. (4) Parts of structural queries can be answered solely based on LIDs. Hence, less information needs to be stored in the index. This potentially decreases the required I/O bandwidth. (5) Additional I/O is needed to retrieve the result nodes of the query.

We now turn our attention to index-based QEPs in which we reorder location steps. We treat the reordering of location steps separately because there are two main issues that limit the value of join reordering for XPath expressions: (1) Join ordering in general is known to be NP hard. When we allow to sort by document order at the end, the search space contains $O((2n)!/n!)$ bushy join trees and $O(n!)$ left deep join trees [24,25,22] containing n joins. Here, we consider one scan for each location step and include cross products. (2) The quality of the generated plans heavily depends on the precision of cardinality estimates [19].

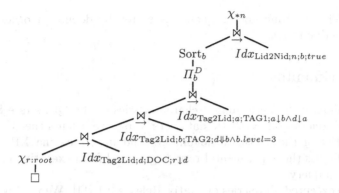

Fig. 5. Plan with index access reordered

However, good methods for cardinality estimation are known only for restricted classes of XPath [26,30].

The reordered translation is shown in Fig. 5. There are three differences to the previous plan: (1) We reordered the axis steps. (2) The residual predicates had to be adjusted. (3) To establish the document order, we need a final sort.

The potential value of reordering axis steps stems from the possibility of evaluating axis steps with low result cardinality first to minimize the number of lookup operations in the index. The additional freedom of reordering location steps has to be payed with an additional sort operation (which is always needed now) and less restrictive structural predicates. Hence, it is not clear which strategy is better in which case. In general, this decision should be based on costs.

4.3   Plan Using Index and Structural Join

The plans discussed in the previous section access the index for each context node. Thanks to the Structural Join, we can evaluate a location step with a single scan of each input and we still have full the freedom to choose the most efficient plan among all bushy join constructed with Structural Joins [6,29].

One possible QEP using Structural Joins is depicted in Fig. 6. In this plan, a Structural Join is performed between the nodes with tag name TAG1 and TAG2. Since both input sequences are sorted in document order, the Structural Join can compute its result with one scan through both sequences and some additional

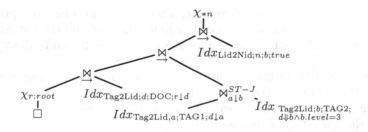

Fig. 6. Plan using index and Structural Join

buffering. The resulting node sequence is sorted by document order and does not produce duplicates.

5 Experiments

We now compare the performance characteristics of the QEPs (see Sec. 4) for three XPath queries on synthetic data sets. First, we discuss the structure and characteristics of the synthetic documents and introduce the XPath queries. Then, we discuss the experimental results gathered from executing each type of QEP on each query.

We have executed all queries on Natix Release 2.1 [11]. We used a buffer size of 8MB. Each query was executed three times with cold buffer. We report the average of all three evaluations. Our execution environment was a PC with two 3GHz Intel Xeon CPUs, 1 GB of RAM, 34GB hard disc (FUJITSU MAS3367NC) running SUSE Linux with kernel 2.6.11-smp.

5.1 Data Set

To get precise performance characteristics for each of the evaluation strategies, the queries access generated data sets. This allows us to tune the selectivity of each XPath location step individually.

The input documents used in our experiments were generated by the XDG document generator implemented by our group.[1] It allows to specify several parameters, i.e. the number of nodes, the document depth, the fan-out of each element, and the number of different tag names.

Conceptually, the generator creates as many child nodes as defined by the parameter "Fan-out" and resumes with a recursive call for each child. When the depth of the recursive calls reaches the specified parameter value "Depth", no recursive calls are executed any more. The frequency of occurrences of tag names decreases by a factor 2 for each subsequent tag name. E.g. the argument "C" for parameter "Elements" means that the tag names A, B, and C are used in the document where every second node gets tag name A, every fourth node gets tag name B, and so on. To get up to 100%, nodes with tag name A are generated. In our setup this means that exactly 50.1% of the nodes are A nodes. The tool generates new nodes until the limit for the number of nodes (#Nodes) is reached.

In principle, this generator might introduce correlations between predicates such that the distribution of tag names strongly depends on the parent nodes. For our data sets this is not the case for tag names A, B, C, and D. However, the remaining tag names only occur as leaf nodes.

We generated documents of four sizes with the parameters summarized in Fig. 7. In this figure, we give the size of the generated text. This setup allows us to control the selectivity of each location step between 50% and 0.1% by changing the name test of each location step.

---

[1] Available for download at http://db.informatik.uni-mannheim.de/xdg.html

Document Parameter		Document Instance			
Parameter	Description	0.327MB	3.46MB	36.5MB	384MB
#Nodes	# of generated XML elements	10,000	100,000	1,000,000	10,000,000
Depth	max. depth of the document	4	5	6	7
Fan-out	# of children per element node		10		
Elements	# of different tag names		"J" (10)		

Fig. 7. Parameters and characteristics of generated documents

5.2   XPath Queries

We have compared the performance characteristics of the QEPs discussed in Sec. 4 for the following three XPath query patterns:

Q1: /descendant::TAG. This query reveals the impact of the access patterns of the QEPs because when evaluating this query structural information is unimportant. The navigational plan visits the whole document to access all potential result nodes. In contrast, the index-based plans only visit specific parts of the document, i.e. those including nodes with tag name TAG.

The main difference is that the navigational plan performs random I/O in the worst case, whereas the index-based QEP can directly retrieve the requested nodes by a range scan on the "Tag2Lid" index.

Q2: /DOC/TAG1/TAG2. With this query we investigate (1) how well each plan alternative exploits structural properties demanded by the query, and (2) how reordering navigation steps effects query performance.

Q3: /DOC/descendant::TAG1/descendant::TAG2. In addition to query Q2, the cost of evaluating each step in this query is potentially much higher because level information is less useful here. As both descendant axis steps potentially visit large parts of the document, we expect optimizations that can reduce the I/O involved here to be very important.

We restrict ourselves to the child axis and the descendent axis because only for these two axes precise selectivity estimation techniques are known, e.g. [30,26]. To make our experimental results comprehensible, we ignore the other XPath axes because we cannot easily compute the selectivity of an axis step with respect to some arbitrary context node.

5.3   Experimental Results

Query Q1. Fig. 8 shows the results for query Q1. In Figs. 8(a) and 8(b) we compare the performance of the navigational plan and the index-based plan for two document sizes, i.e. 3.46MB and 384MB.

For small selectivities on the smaller document, the index-based plan performs better than the navigational plan. As we make the node test less selective, the index-based approach needs more time to evaluate the query while the execution time of the navigational plan remains nearly constant. The break-even is reached

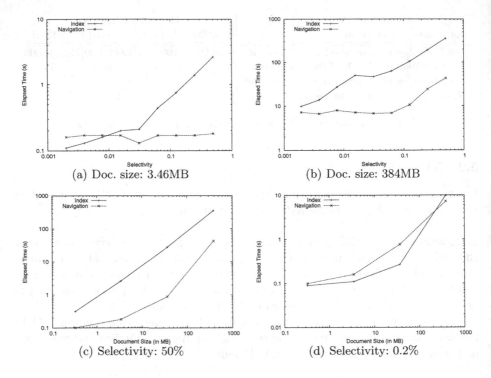

Fig. 8. Query Q1 (/descendant::TAG)

at a selectivity of about 1%. For larger selectivities, the navigational plan out-performs the index-based plan. All these results agree with our experience in the relational world.

In Figs. 8(c) and 8(d) we plot the query execution times for specific selectivities of 50% and 0.2% over varying document sizes.

Again, the results confirm that index-based evaluation is superior only for selective queries. However, since two indices and the document are accessed, more buffer pages have to replaced due to lack of space, and additional I/O is needed. As a result, the performance of the index-based plan suffers on the largest document instance.

Query Q2. Fig. 9 contains the results of our experiments for query Q2. We restrict ourselves to two document sizes (3.46MB and 384MB) because the results on the other documents do not provide any additional insight. In our exposition we keep the selectivity of the second location step (**TAG2**) constant at 50% (see Figs. 9(a) and 9(c)) and at 0.2% (see Figs. 9(b) and 9(d)). We only modified the selectivity of the first location step (**TAG1**).

The navigational QEP has an almost constant execution time independent of the selectivity. This is a direct consequence of its evaluation strategy: this QEP has to inspect the same set of nodes to compute its result, no matter how selective each step is. The navigational QEP dominates all other QEPs because

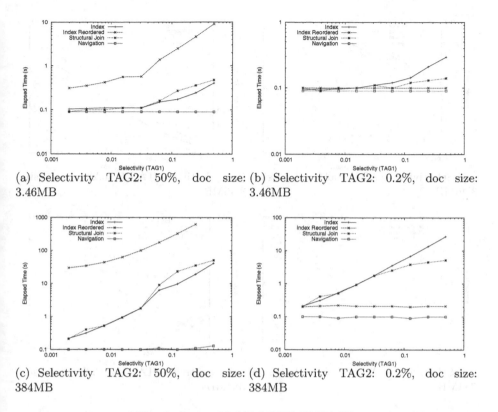

(a) Selectivity TAG2: 50%, doc size: 3.46MB

(b) Selectivity TAG2: 0.2%, doc size: 3.46MB

(c) Selectivity TAG2: 50%, doc size: 384MB

(d) Selectivity TAG2: 0.2%, doc size: 384MB

Fig. 9. Query Q2 (/DOC/TAG1/TAG2)

it effectively prunes the document fragments that are not relevant for the query result. This holds true particularly for the deeply nested document where this plan only visits the three upper levels of the document.

The value of reordering location steps becomes apparent when we compare the execution times of the naive and the reordered version of the index-based plans. In the experiments depicted in Figs. 9(a) and 9(c), the reordered version is up to ten times slower than the naive plan because the reordered QEP performs the more expensive scan first (selectivity 50%). In Figs. 9(b) and 9(d) we observe exactly the reverse behavior because the second location step is very selective (selectivity = 0.2%). However, the differences are smaller because the naive plan can use more information to restrict the index scan. In all experiments the Structural Join behaves similar to the naive index-based evaluation technique. The index based technique is competitive because none of the navigation steps produces duplicates. Hence, no redundant index lookup is performed.

The advantage of the navigational plan is partially a consequence of the document structure. For shallow documents where we increase the number of children per node, we expect similar behavior as for query Q3.

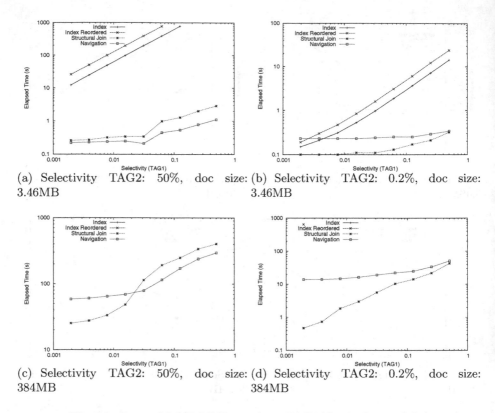

(a) Selectivity TAG2: 50%, doc size: 3.46MB

(b) Selectivity TAG2: 0.2%, doc size: 3.46MB

(c) Selectivity TAG2: 50%, doc size: 384MB

(d) Selectivity TAG2: 0.2%, doc size: 384MB

Fig. 10. Query Q3 (/DOC/descendant::TAG1/descendant::TAG2)

Query Q3. For our final experiment, we replace the last two child steps of Q2 by descendant steps: `/DOC/descendant::TAG1/descendant::TAG2`. The execution times for these three alternatives are shown in Fig. 10. We present the results for the same selectivities and document sizes as the figures for query Q2 do.

First, we discuss the navigational approach: We observe that in all figures the evaluation times of the navigational QEP increase with an increasing selectivity of the name tests. The reason for this is that the XPath expression generates more context nodes for which the whole subtree is traversed. For larger selectivities, fewer subtrees are pruned during the traversal.

In contrast, the index-based QEPs retrieve exactly the candidate nodes with the correct tag name. However, only in Fig. 10(b) both index-based strategies are faster than navigation for very small selectivities on a small document. The reason for this is that our naive index-based execution strategy is not aware of structural relationships of context nodes. As a result, the same nodes are returned repeatedly by index lookups. We conclude that the simple index-based QEPs do not result in an acceptable query performance.

Fortunately, the plan based on Structural Joins avoids these superfluous index lookups. For large selectivities (of 50%) of the second step, the Structural Join is faster when the selectivity of the first step is smaller than about 2% and the document is large (Fig. 10(c)). However, when we keep the selectivity of the second step at 0.2%, the Structural Join clearly outperforms the navigational query independent of the selectivity of the first step and the document size. This advantage is larger when the selectivity of the location steps are small.

6 Conclusion and Future Work

There are many possibilities to optimize XPath expressions. Several indexing and evaluation techniques have been proposed. However, we still lack cost-based optimizers that compare alternative query evaluation plans based on costs. As a starting point, we have compared two basic evaluation techniques: navigation-based and index-based XPath evaluation.

Our experiments show that there is no overall winner: Each technique has its individual strengths and weaknesses. In general, navigation is a good choice when large parts of the input document belong to the query result or when navigation can avoid visiting large parts of the document. Unfortunately, there is no simple rule where the break-even point between both alternatives lies. However, a selectivity of about 1% to 10% for elements of a given tag name still seem to be decisive when navigation must be traded against index usage. For space reasons, we could only compare a limited number of evaluation techniques. Certainly other query evaluation techniques should be included into benchmarking, e.g. see [23].

In previous work, sophisticated cardinality estimation techniques were developed for the child axis and the descendent axis. We need to extend these results and the results of this paper to include cost information. Using statistics or analyzing the query processing algorithms are possibilities to achieve this goal. We then could integrate XQuery processing techniques into cost-based query optimizers and overcome using heuristics as is currently the case.

Acknowledgements. We would like to thank the anonymous referees who noticed a weak spot in our experiments and thus helped us to improve our query evaluation plans. We also thank Simone Seeger for her comments on the manuscript.

References

1. M. Brantner, C-C. Kanne, S. Helmer, and G. Moerkotte. Full-fledged algebraic XPath processing in Natix. In *Proc. ICDE*, pages 705–716, 2005.
2. S. Chien, Z. Vagena, D. Zhang, V. J. Tsotras, and C. Zaniolo. Efficient structural joins on indexed XML documents. In *Proc. VLDB*, pages 263–274, 2002.
3. E. Cohen, H. Kaplan, and T. Milo. Labeling dynamic XML trees. In *Proc. of the ACM PODS*, pages 271–281, 2002.
4. A. Deutsch, M. Fernandez, and D. Suciu. Storing semistructured data with STORED. In *Proc. of the ACM SIGMOD*, pages 431–442, 1999.
5. A. Halverson et al. Mixed mode XML query processing. In *Proc. VLDB*, pages 225–236, 2003.
6. D. Srivastava et al. Structural joins: A primitive for efficient XML query pattern matching. In *Proc. ICDE*, pages 141–152, 2002.

7. F. Ozcan et al. System RX: One part relational, one part XML. In *Proc. of the ACM SIGMOD*, pages 347–358, 2005.
8. H. Jagadish et al. Timber: A native XML database. *VLDB Journal*, 11(4):274–291, December 2002.
9. P. E. O'Neil et al. ORDPATHs: Insert-friendly XML node labels. In *Proc. of the ACM SIGMOD*, pages 903–908, 2004.
10. S. Pal et al. XQuery implementation in a relational database system. In *Proc. VLDB*, pages 1175–1186, 2005.
11. T. Fiebig et al. Anatomy of a native XML base management system. *VLDB Journal*, 11(4):292–314, December 2002. available at: http://db.informatik.uni-mannheim.de/natix.html.
12. R. Goldman and J. Widom. DataGuides: Enabling query formulation and optimization in semistructured databases. In *Proc. VLDB*, pages 436–445, 1997.
13. G. Graefe. Query evaluation techniques for large databases. *ACM Computing Surveys*, 25(2):73–170, June 1993.
14. J. Gray and G. Graefe. The five-minute rule ten years later, and other computer storage rules of thumb. *SIGMOD Record*, 26(4):63–68, 1997.
15. T. Grust. Accelerating XPath location steps. In *Proc. of the ACM SIGMOD*, pages 109–120, 2002.
16. T. Grust, M. van Keulen, and J. Teubner. Staircase join: Teach a relational DBMS to watch its (axis) steps. In *Proc. VLDB*, pages 524–525, 2003.
17. S. Helmer, C-C. Kanne, and G. Moerkotte. Optimized translation of XPath expressions into algebraic expressions parameterized by programs containing navigational primitives. In *Proc. of WISE*, pages 215–224, 2002.
18. J. Hidders and P. Michiels. Avoiding unnecessary ordering operations in XPath. In *DBPL*, pages 54–74, 2003.
19. Y. E. Ioannidis and S. Christodoulakis. On the propagation of errors in the size of join results. In *Proc. of the ACM SIGMOD*, pages 268–277, 1991.
20. I. Jaluta, S. Sippu, and E. Soisalon-Soininen. Concurrency control and recovery for balanced B-link trees. *VLDB Journal*, 14(2):257–277, 2005.
21. Q. Li and B. Moon. Indexing and querying XML data for regular path expressions. In *Proc. VLDB*, pages 361–370, 2001.
22. N. May, S. Helmer, C-C. Kanne, and G. Moerkotte. XQuery processing in Natix with an emphasis on join ordering. In $< XIME - P/ >$, pages 49–54, 2004.
23. P. Michiels, G. A. Mihăilă, and J. Siméon. Put a tree pattern in your algebra. Technical report, Univ. of Antwerp, TR-06-09, Belgium, 2006.
24. K. Ono and G. Lohman. Measuring the complexity of join enumeration in query optimization. In *Proc. VLDB*, pages 314–325, 1990.
25. A. Pellenkoft, C. Galindo-Legaria, and M. Kersten. The complexity of transformation-based join enumeration. In *Proc. VLDB*, pages 306–315, 1997.
26. N. Polyzotis and M. Garofalakis. XCluster synopses for structured XML content. In *Proc. ICDE*, pages 406–507, 2006.
27. C. Re, J. Simeon, and M. Fernandez. A complete and efficient algebraic compiler for XQuery. In *Proc. ICDE*, pages 138–149, 2006.
28. F. Tian, D. DeWitt, J. Chen, and C. Zhang. The design and performance evaluation of alternative XML storage strategies. *SIGMOD Record*, 31(1), 2002.
29. Y. Wu, J. Patel, and H. Jagadish. Structural join order selection for XML query optimization. In *Proc. ICDE*, pages 443–454, 2003.
30. N. Zhang, T. Özsu, A. Aboulnaga, and I. F. Alyas. XSeed: Accurate and fast cardinality estimation for XPath queries. In *Proc. ICDE*, pages 168–179, 2006.

Consistency of Temporal XML Documents

Marcela Campo[1] and Alejandro Vaisman[2]

[1] Universidad de Buenos Aires
mcampo@dc.uba.ar
[2] Universidad de Chile
avaisman@dcc.uchile.cl

Abstract. Different models have been recently proposed for representing temporal data, tracking historical information, and recovering the state of the document as of any given time, in XML documents. After presenting an abstract model for temporal XML, we discuss the problem of the validation of the temporal constraints imposed by this model. We first review the problem of checking and fixing isolated temporal inconsistencies. Then, we move on to study validation of a document when many temporal inconsistencies of different kinds are present. We study the conditions that allow to treat each inconsistency isolated from the rest, and give the corresponding proofs. These properties are intended to be the basis of efficient algorithms for checking temporal consistency in XML.

1 Introduction

The problem of validating an XML document with respect to a set of integrity constraints after an update occurs, has recently attracted the attention of the database community. Many incremental validation techniques have been proposed [2,3,10,14]. In the temporal XML setting, although several models exist for representing, querying and updating temporal information [1,5,7,8], little attention has been given to the problem of validating the temporal constraints imposed by these models. In Temporal XML documents, the updates must take as input (and return) a valid XML document, not only with respect to the usual set of integrity constraints, but also with respect to the temporal constraints defined by the model at hand. Further, more often than not, we will not be working with documents built from scratch using update operations, but with a pre-existent temporal XML document; thus, we will need to efficiently check if this document verifies a set of temporal constraints, and, if not, provide the user with tools for fixing the inconsistencies, if needed.

In this work we address the problem of validating a set of temporal constraints in a temporal XML document. Although our proposal is based in the data model introduced in [12] (discussed in more detail in Section 3), it could be extended to other data models for temporal XML. After presenting and discussing the data model, we characterize temporal inconsistencies in temporal XML documents. We then introduce the problem of checking inconsistencies in a document, and fixing individual inconsistencies. Then, we move on to a more realistic scenario,

S. Amer-Yahia et al. (Eds.): XSym 2006, LNCS 4156, pp. 31–45, 2006.

where many inconsistencies could appear concurrently, and study the conditions under which these inconsistencies could be teated isolated from each other. These properties could then be embedded in efficient algorithms for fixing inconsistencies in temporal XML documents. To the best of our knowledge, this is the first contribution in this topic.

The remainder of the paper is organized as follows: in Section 2 we review previous efforts in temporal semistructured/XML data. In Section 3 we introduce the temporal data model. Section 4 presents the main kinds of inconsistencies that may appear in a temporal XML document, and discusses how they can be fixed. Section 5 addresses documents where more than one consistency condition is violated. We conclude in Section 6.

2   Related Work

Some proposals have been recently presented addressing incremental validation of XML documents. Kane *et al* [10] model XML constraints as rules, and present a constraint checking mechanism for update operations, aimed at ensuring that the result of an update leaves the XML document in a consistent state. Basically, this is performed by rewriting an update query into a so-called *safe update* query. Incremental validation of XML documents has also been studied in [2,3,14].

Chawathe *et al* proposed a historical model for *semistructured data* [4], that extends the Object Exchange Model (OEM) with the ability to represent updates and to keep track of them by means of "deltas". Along the same lines, Oliboni *et al* [13] proposed a graphical data model and query language for semistructured data. Both works assume that the documents are consistent with respect to the temporal constraints the models impose. Several data models for *Temporal XML* have been proposed. All of them lack of a mechanism for checking the underlying temporal constraints. In contrast, in this paper we study different ways of tackling (temporal) consistency in temporal XML documents. Amagasa *et al* [1] introduced a temporal data model based in XPath, but not a model for updates, nor a query language taking advantage of the temporal model. Dyreson [7] proposed an extension of XPath with support for transaction time by means of the addition of several temporal axes for specifying temporal directions. Chien *et al* [5] proposed update and versioning schemes for XML, through a scheme where version management is performed by keeping references to the maximal unchanged subtree in the previous version. A similar approach was also followed by Marian *et al* [11]. Gao *et al* [8] introduced τXQuery, an extension to XQuery supporting valid time while maintaining the data model unchanged. Queries are translated into XQuery, and evaluated by an XQuery engine. Finally, Wang *et al* have also proposed solutions based in versioning [16]. In this paper we will work over a data model first introduced in [12].

3   Temporal XML Documents

We will introduce the model through an example, depicted in Figure 1. This is an abstract representation of a temporal XML document for a portion of a

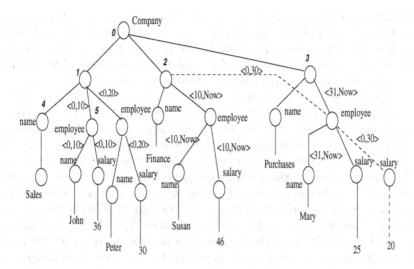

Fig. 1. Example database

company involving departments and their employees. The database also records salaries and, probably, other properties of the employees. Note that in this model, employee's nodes are not duplicated throughout time. For example, can see that John and Peter worked for the Sales department in the intervals [0,10] and [0,20] respectively, while Susan has been working for the Finance department since instant "10". When an edge has no temporal label, its validity interval is assumed to be [0,Now] (i.e. the complete lifespan of the node). Thus, the abstract representation of the temporal document presented in Figure 1 contains the whole history of the company. We can then query the state of the database at a certain point in time, or pose temporal queries like "employees who worked for the Sales department continuously since the year 2000." In [12] the authors provided indexing schemes allowing efficient query evaluation techniques.

More formally, an XML document is a directed labeled graph, where we distinguish several classes of nodes: (a) a distinguished node r, the *root* of the document, such that r has no incoming edges, and every node in the graph is reachable from r; (b) *Value nodes*: nodes representing values (text or numeric); they have no outgoing edges, and have exactly one incoming edge, from attribute or element nodes (or from the root); (c) *Attribute nodes*: labeled with the name of an attribute, plus possibly one of the 'ID' or 'REF' annotations; (d) *Element nodes:* labeled with an element tag, and containing outgoing links to attribute nodes, value nodes, and other element nodes. Each node is uniquely identified by an integer, the *node number,* and is described by a string, the *node label*. Edges in the document graph are constrained to be either *containment edges* or *reference edges*. A containment edge $e_c(n_i, n_j)$ joins two nodes n_i and n_j such that n_i is either r or an element node, and n_j is an attribute node, a value node or another element node; a reference edge $e_r(n_i, n_j)$ links an attribute node n_i of type REF, with an element node n_j. We add the time dimension to document graphs labeling edges with intervals. We will consider time as a discrete, linearly ordered domain. An ordered pair $[a, b]$ of time points, with $a \leq b$, denotes the closed interval from a to b. As usual in temporal databases, the current time point will be represented with the distinguished word '*Now*'. The document's creation instant will be indistinctly denoted by the instant "$0''$".

A *temporal label* over a a containment edge $e_c(n_i, n_j)$, is an interval T_{e_c} representing the time period when the element represented by n_j was contained in the element represented by n_i. Our model supports *transaction time* of the containment relation. Although we do not deal with *valid time*, it could be addressed in an analogous way. Analogously, for reference edges, T_{e_r} represents the *transaction* time of the reference edge $e_r(n_i, n_j)$. We note that the full model supports other kinds of nodes, like *versioned* and *attribute* nodes, that we will not consider here. We will use $T_e.TO$ and $T_e.FROM$ to refer to the endpoints of the interval T_e. Two temporal labels T_{e_i} and T_{e_j} are *consecutive* if $T_{e_j}.FROM = T_{e_i}.TO + 1$. The *lifespan* of a node is the union of the temporal labels of all the containment edges incoming to the node. The lifespan of the root is the interval $[t_0, Now]$.

Definition 1 (Temporal XML Document). *A* Temporal XML Document *is a document graph, augmented with temporal labels and versioned nodes, that satisfies the following conditions: (1) The union of the temporal labels of the containment edges outgoing from a node is contained in the lifespan of the node. (2) The temporal labels of the containment edges incoming to a node are consecutive. (3) For any time instant t, the sub-graph composed by all containment edges e_c such that $t \in T_{e_c}$ is a tree with root* r, *called the* snapshot *of $\mathcal{D}$ at time t, denoted $\mathcal{D}(t)$. (4) For any containment edge $e_c(n_i, n_j, T_{e_c})$, if n_j is a node of type ID, the time label of e_c is the same as the lifespan of n_i; moreover, if there are two elements in the document with the same value for an ID attribute, both elements are the same. In other words, the ID of a node remains constant for all the snapshots of the document. (5) For any containment edge $e_c(n_i, n_j, T_{e_c})$, if n_j is an attribute of type REF, such that there exists a reference edge $e_r(n_j, n_k, T_r)$, then $T_{e_c} = T_{e_r}$ holds. (6) Given a reference edge $e_r(n_i, n_j, T_{e_r})$, $T_{e_r} \subseteq l_{n_j}$ holds.*

Note that the second condition in Definition 1 implies that we will be working with single intervals instead of temporal elements. This assumption simplifies the presentation and makes the implementations more efficient, although it imposes some constraints on the model. Our definitions and theorems can be, however, extended to the case of temporal elements, overriding the former limitation. Discussion on this topic, and a more detailed description of the model, can be found in [12]. We will also need the following definition:

Definition 2 (Continuous Path and Maximal Continuous Path). *A continuous path* with interval T *from node n_1 to node n_k in a temporal document graph is a sequence $(n_1, \ldots, n_k, T)$ of k nodes and an interval T such that there is a sequence of containment edges of the form $e_1(n_1, n_2, T_1)$, $e_2(n_2, n_3, T_2)$, $\ldots$, $e_k(n_{k-1}, n_k, T_k)$, such that $T = \bigcap_{i=1,k} T_i$. We say there is a maximal* *continuous path (mcp) with interval T from node n_1 to node n_k if T is the union of a maximal set of consecutive intervals T_i such that there is a continuous path from n_1 to n_k with interval T_i.*

4   Consistency in Temporal XML

In this section we will summarize previous results on the problem of checking consistency, and fixing isolated inconsistencies. Details can be found in [15]. In addition, we will give the definitions and concepts needed for studying the general problem (i.e., multiple inconsistencies), that we discuss in the next section.

Definition 3 (Inconsistencies in Temporal XML). *The constraints stated in Definition 1 are violated if: (i) there is an outgoing containment edge whose temporal label is outside the node's lifespan; (ii) the temporal labels of the containment edges incoming to a node are not consecutive. Here, the inconsistency may be due to a gap or an overlapping of the temporal labels of the edges incoming to a node; (iii) there is a cycle in some document's snapshot; (iv) there exist more than one node with the same value for the ID attribute. We will denote these types of inconsistencies as inconsistencies of type i, type ii, type iii, and type iv. An* Interval of Inconsistency*, denoted I_I is the closed interval where consistency conditions in Definition 3 are not satisfied.*

As we will only consider temporal issues in this paper, we will only study inconsistencies of types i through iii. Also, we will work with documents containing no IDREF or IDREFS attributes.

Example 1. Figures 2 (a) to (c) show examples of inconsistencies of types i through iii, and their intervals. In Figure 2(a) $I_I = [T_4, Now]$; in Figure 2 (b) $I_I = [T_2, T_4]$; in Figure 2 (c) there is a cycle in every snapshot within the interval $I_I = [T_4, T_6]$.

Checking Consistency. Inconsistencies of types i and ii are checked using the function $lifespan(n)$, that, given a node n computes its lifespan. For inconsistencies of type i, the algorithm checks, for each edge e, if T_e is in $lifespan(n)$. If there is an inconsistency of type ii, $lifespan(n)$ returns $null$. It can be shown that the lifespan of a node can be computed with an order $O(deg_{in}(n)* log(deg_{in}(n)))$, where $deg_{in}(n)$ is the number of edges incident to n. In the worst case (where all edges in the graph are incident to the node), the order of the algorithm is $O(|E| * log(|E|))$; in the average case (all nodes have the same number of incoming edges, i.e. $\frac{|E|}{|V|}$), this reduces to $O(\frac{|E|}{|V|} * log(\frac{|E|}{|V|}))$. In the best case (when each node has only one incoming edge) the lifespan is computed in constant time.

Inconsistencies of type iii are checked (with order $O(|E| + |V|)$) using the following proposition.

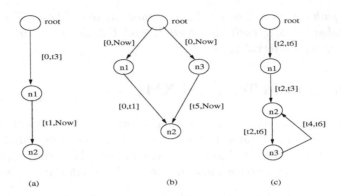

Fig. 2. (a) Inconsistency of type i; (b) Inconsistency of type ii; (c) Inconsistency of type iii

Proposition 1. *Let D be a Temporal XML document where every node has at most one incoming containment edge in every time instant t; if there is a cycle in some interval I_I in D, then, there exists a node n_i such that $T_{mcp}(n_i) \neq lifespan(n_i)$, where $T_{mcp(n_i)}$ is the temporal interval of the mcp between the root and node n_i.*

Definition 4 (Deleting edges). *Let D be a Temporal XML document, and let e be a containment edge $e(n_i, n_j, T_e)$. We define three different kinds of deletion of containment edges: (1) Physical Delete of an edge e is the deletion of e during all the edge's lifespan. (2) Delete e in an instant $t \in Te$, with three variants: (a) Physical delete e, if $T_e.FROM = T_e.TO = t$; (b) make $T_e.TO = t - 1$, if $T_e.TO = t \wedge T_e.FROM < t$; (c) make $T_e.TO = t+1$, if $T_e.TO = t \wedge T_e.FROM > t$; (d) Create a duplicate of n_j at instant t, and delete e in t (see below) if $T_e.FROM < t < T_e.TO$. (3) Delete e in an Interval I is the deletion of the edge e for each instant $t, t \in I \cap T_e$.*

Duplication of a node n at instant t_d is performed as follows: (1) create a new node n_c, and, for all edges $e_j(n, n_i, T_{e_j})$ outgoing from n, create a new edge $e_k(n_c, n_i, T_{e_j})$; (2) delete (following Definition 4), all edges outgoing from n, for all instant $t \geq t_d$; (3) delete all edges outgoing from n_c, for all instant $t < t_d$; (4) for each edge $e_i(n_i, n, T_{e_i})$ incident to n such that $T_{e_i}.TO \geq t$ create a new edge $e_n(n_i, n_c, T_{n_i})$ with $T_{n_i}.FROM = t$ if $t \in T_{n_i}$, and $T_{n_i} = T_{e_i}$ otherwise; (5) finally, delete all edges e_i in the interval $[t, T_{e_i}.TO]$ if $t \in T_{e_i}$. It can be shown node duplication can be performed in $O(deg_{out}(n) + deg_{in}(n)) \approx O(|E|)$ time.

The first kind of deletion in Definition 4 is a physical deletion, that is, the whole edge disappears. The second kind of deletion has different flavors. If the edge is deleted in an instant that corresponds to a boundary of it interval of validity (T_e), this boundary is incremented (decremented) in one time unit. Finally, if the edge is deleted in an instant inside T_e, the target node of the edge is split into two, as explained above. Deletion during an interval is just a straightforward generalization of the above.

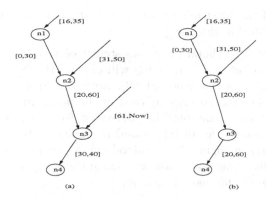

Fig. 3. Inconsistency of type i

Definition 5 (Temporal Label Expansion and Reduction). *Given a containment edge* $e(n_i, n_j, T_e)$, *an expansion of* T_e *to an instant* t *is performed making* $T_e.TO = t$, *if* $t > T_e.TO$, *and* $T_e.FROM = t$, *if* $t < T_e.FROM$.

Analogously, reducing the temporal label T_e *to an interval* $T' \subset T_e$ *implies deleting e in the intervals* $[T_e.FROM, T'.FROM - 1], [T'.TO + 1, T_e.TO]$.

Given two intervals T_1 and T_1, if $T_1.TO > T_2.TO$ we will say that T_1 is *greater than* T_2, denoted $T_1 \succ T_2$. Analogously, if $T_1.TO < T_2.TO$, we say that T_1 *precedes* T_2, denoted $T_1 \prec T_2$.

Definition 6 (Youngest (Oldest) Incoming Edge). *We will denote youngest edge incoming to a node* n, $y_e(n)$, *an edge whose temporal label is the largest (according to the definition above) among all the temporal labels of the edges incoming to* n. *Analogously we define the oldest edge incoming to a node* n, $o_e(n)$, *as an edge whose temporal label is less than the labels of all the other edges incoming to* n.

Fixing Inconsistencies of Type i. We study two ways of fixing the problem: (a) correction by expansion; and (b) correction by reduction. *Correction by expansion* expands the lifespan of the inconsistent node until it covers the violating interval; for this task, if $I_I \succ lifespan(n)$, $y_e(n)$ (i.e., the youngest incoming edge) is chosen for expansion; if $lifespan(n) \succ I_I$, $o_e(n)$ is chosen. The problem with this solution is twofold: on the one hand, we do not really know if the containment relation actually existed in the new interval. An expert user will be needed to define this. On the other hand, the expansion may introduce a cycle (i.e., an inconsistency of type iii). In this case, expansion will not be a possible solution. *Correction by reduction* shrinks the temporal label of the inconsistent edge, in order to close I_I. The main idea here is to modify the temporal label of the inconsistent edge, in order that it lies within the lifespan of the starting node of such edge. Although no cycle can be introduced by this solution, new inconsistencies of type i may appear in the ending node of the modified edge, if this node has outgoing edges that cover the interval that has to be reduced; moreover, inconsistencies of type ii may also be introduced if the deleted interval was not in one of the lifespan's extremes. Finally, note that reduction can be propagated downward in cascade.

Example 2. Figure 3(a) shows an inconsistency of type i at node n_2, where $I_I = [51, 60]$. A *correction by expansion* will expand the youngest edge incoming to n_2, resulting in a new label $[31, 60]$. Note that an expansion may recursively propagate the inconsistency upward in the path, until a consistent state is reached. In the same example, the *correction by reduction* approach would generate new inconsistencies of type i and ii. Reducing to $[20,50]$ the interval of the edge (n_2, n_3) in Figure 3 (a), introduces a gap in node n_3. In the case of Figure 3 (b), the same correction will make the temporal label of the edge (n_3, n_4) lie outside the lifespan of node n_3.

Fixing Inconsistencies of Type ii. In this case we have two possibilities: (a) there is an overlapping of some of the temporal labels incoming to a node; (b) the union of the temporal labels of the edges incoming to a node presents a gap.

For fixing overlapping it suffices just to delete one of the violating edges in the interval of inconsistency. Closing the gaps has more than one possible solution: (a) physically delete all incoming edges occurring after the gap (i.e., with temporal labels starting after the gap); (b) expand the temporal labels of the edges, in order to close the gap (this could be performed expanding the temporal labels of one or more of the edges involved); (c) duplicate the violating node in a way such that the resulting incoming and outgoing edges have consistent temporal labels. The first two options may introduce new inconsistencies of type i (for example, if the violating node is n, there is an edge $e(n_i, n, T_e)$, and T_e is expanded to T_e', the latter label may be outside the lifespan of n_i). The third option requires the node created to be semantically equivalent and syntactically consistent. Fixing inconsistencies of type ii can be done in $O(|E|)^2$ time [15].

Fixing Inconsistencies of Type iii. Inconsistencies of type iii involve cycles occurring in some interval(s) of the document's lifespan. In this case, again, we have more than one possible way of fixing the inconsistency, basically consisting in deleting (according to Definition 4) edges within the cycle. We may (a) delete all containment edges involved in a cycle during the inconsistency interval I_I (i.e., the interval when the cycle occurs); or (b) delete (within the interval of inconsistency) one of the edges in the cycle. Given that this would introduce an inconsistency of type i, this solution is only possible if there is at least one node n in the cycle with more than one incoming containment edge $e_c(n_i, n, T_e)$, such that T_e lies outside I_I. Thus, besides deleting the edge, T_e must be expanded in order to prevent introducing a new inconsistence.

5   Interaction Between Inconsistencies

So far we have studied document inconsistencies isolated from each other. In a real-world scenario, it is likely that more than one inconsistency appears in a document. In this section we tackle this problem. First, we need some definitions.

Definition 7 (Expansion paths). *We denote* youngest parent of a node n, *the origin node of* $y_e(n)$. *The* oldest parent of a node *is the origin node of* $o_e(n)$. *A path of oldest (youngest) parents between two nodes* n_i, n_j *is a path where each node is the youngest (oldest) parent of the next node in the path. We will denote these paths* expansion paths.

Definition 8 (Area of Influence). *We will call* Area of Influence *of an inconsistency* I, *denoted* $A_{inf}(I)$, *the union of all the nodes affected by the possible solutions to the inconsistencies studied in Section 4. An affected node is a node changed as a consequence of fixing an inconsistency, i.e., a node such that (a) an incoming or outgoing node was deleted; (b) a temporal label of an incoming or outgoing edge was expanded or reduced.*

For an inconsistency I of type i, the *Area of Influence of I* is the set of nodes composed of: the inconsistent node n, all the nodes in the expansion paths of n, and all the nodes n_i in the document such that there is a continuous path from n to n_i during I_{I_i} (the interval of inconsistency of I).

The *Area of Influence of an Inconsistency of type ii* is only composed of the inconsistent node n. Given that the solution for this kind of inconsistency is the duplication of the node, only the edges are affected (and a new node will be created).

The *Area of Influence of an Inconsistency of Type iii* during an Interval of Inconsistency I_I is composed of: (a) all the nodes n_i in the cycle (*corresponds to the solution of deleting all nodes in the cycle*); (b) all nodes n_j such that there is a continuous path from n_i to n_j with interval $T \supseteq I_{I_{iii}}$ (*a consequence of the above*); (c) all the nodes in the expansion path of each node in the cycle, with temporal label less than I_I; (corresponds to the solution of deleting only one edge in the cycle).

Example 3. Figure 4 (a) shows an example of an inconsistency of type i over node n_3. The possible solutions are, as we have seen before, correction by reduction or by expansion. The former affects all nodes belonging to a path with origin in n_3, in the interval $[t3, t10]$ (i.e., n_4 and n_6). Expansion would affect all nodes in the path of youngest parents of n_3, i.e, n_2 and n_1. Then, the area of influence is the set: $\{n_1, n_2, n_4, n_6, n_3\}$.

Figure 4 (b) depicts the area of influence of a cycle between nodes n_2, n_3, n_4 and n_5. If all of them are deleted, node n_7 will also be affected, because it is reached from n_3 within the cycle's interval. In fact, all nodes, except n_2 will be physically deleted. Deleting only the ending node of one inconsistent edge in the cycle implies deleting node n_2 (we delete $e(n_5, n_2, T_{52})$), expanding the intervals of the path of youngest parents of n_2, i.e., n_1 is also affected.

If more than one inconsistency appears in a temporal XML document, the order in which we solve them will have an impact on the document that we will finally obtain. We would like to identify, at low cost, sets of inconsistencies that do not interfere with each other. In this case, we would be able to fix them in any order, and the result will be the same. The notion of area of influence allows us to identify such sets.

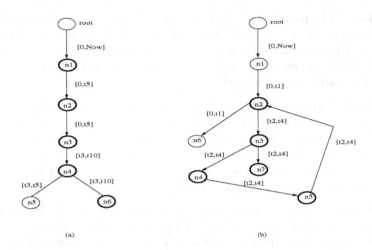

Fig. 4. Inconsistencies of Types i and iii - Area of influence

Intuitively, given any pair of inconsistencies (of any type), I_1 and I_2, we say that I_1 and I_2 *interfere* with each other if their areas of influence have non-empty intersection. Conversely, if $A_{inf}(I_1) \cap A_{inf}(I_2) \neq \phi$, we say that I_1 and I_2 are *isolated* from each other. Given a set of n inconsistencies $I_1, ..., I_n$, we denote the set composed of the nodes in $A_{inf}(I_1) \cap A_{inf}(I_2)... \cap A_{inf}(I_n)$, the *Area of Interference* of $I_1, ..., I_n$, denoted $A_i(I_1, I_2, ...I_n)$

Definition 9 (Classification of Interferences). *Given a set of inconsistencies $\mathcal{I} = \{I_1, ..., I_n\}$ such that $A_{inf}(I_1) \cap A_{inf}(I_2)... \cap A_{inf}(I_n) \neq \phi$ we denote their interference* Irrelevant *if we can fix them in any order and obtain the same result (i.e., everything happens as if they were isolated). On the contrary, if this property does not hold, we denote the interference* relevant.

Example 4. Figure 5 (a) shows two irrelevant inconsistencies of type ii over the same node. In both cases, the solution will be node duplication. However, it is easy to see that the result will be the same, no matter which one we address in the first place. Figure 5 (b) shows a cycle interfering with an inconsistency of type i. The cycle cannot be corrected by expansion because it involves nodes in the potential path of youngest parents of the inconsistency of type i.

In what follows, we will study the conditions that state when an interference is irrelevant. Detecting irrelevant interferences through the propositions below, constitutes the basis of an efficient solution to the problem of fixing a document with multiple temporal inconsistencies. We will not address relevant interferences in this paper.

Irrelevant Interferences. In the propositions below, we will be using a simple metric, namely the number of changes needed to fix an inconsistency, where a change could be: (a) the expansion of an interval; (b) the reduction of an interval;

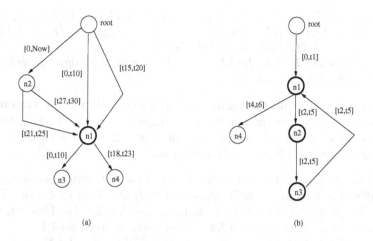

Fig. 5. Relevant and Irrelevant interferences

(c) the duplication of a node; (d) the physical deletion of an edge. For simplicity, we give the same weight to each change. We denote this metric κ. When there is more than one possibility for fixing an inconsistency, this metric will define which method we will use (i.e., the one with the smallest κ). In particular, in Section 4 we proposed two methods for fixing inconsistencies of type i: *correction by expansion* and *correction by reduction*. We denote κ_r and κ_e the number of changes required by a correction by reduction and expansion, respectively.

Definition 10 (Expansion Area). *We call* Expansion Area *of an inconsistency I, denoted $A_e(I)$ the set of nodes belonging to the expansion path(s) that compose the Area of Influence of I. Analogously, we call the* Reduction Area *of I, denoted $A_r(I)$ the set of nodes in all the mcps that compose the Area of Influence of I. It follows that, for inconsistencies of types i and iii, $A_{inf}(I) = A_e(I) \cup A_r(I)$.*

Proposition 2. *Let I_1, I_2 be two inconsistencies of type i, with intervals T_1 and T_2, respectively. If $A_e(I_1) \cap A_r(I_2) = A_e(I_2) \cap A_r(I_1) = \phi$, then, I_1 and I_2 can be solved by expansion, in any order.*

Now, we will give a set of propositions that allows us to determine if two inconsistencies occurring in the same document are irrelevant or not. We will address all possible combinations of inconsistencies, starting from concurrent inconsistencies of the same kind. For the sake of space will only give the proof of some of the propositions.

Proposition 3 (Inconsistencies of type i). *Let I_1, I_2 be two inconsistencies of type i, with intervals T_1 and T_2, respectively. Their interference is irrelevant if at least one of the following holds:*

a. $\kappa_r(I_1) < \kappa_e(I_1) \wedge \kappa_r(I_2) < \kappa_e(I_2) \wedge A_e(I_1) \cup A_r(I_2) = A_e(I_2) \cup A_r(I_1) = \phi$
b. $\kappa_r(I_1) > \kappa_e(I_1) \wedge \kappa_r(I_2) > \kappa_e(I_2) \wedge A_e(I_1) \cup A_r(I_2) = A_e(I_2) \cup A_r(I_1) = \phi$
c. $A_i(I_1, I_2) = A_r(I_1) \cap A_r(I_2) \wedge T_1 \cap T_2 = \phi$.
d. $A_i(I_1, I_2) = A_e(I_1) \cap A_r(I_2) \wedge T_1 \prec T_2$ *(for a path of youngest parents,* $T_1 \succ T_2$
   for a path of oldest parents)

Condition (a) means that the number of changes needed to fix each inconsistency *by reduction* is less than the number of changes required to fix it *by expansion*, and the expansion area of one of them does not intersect with the expansion area of the other. Condition (b) is analogous.

Proof. Condition a. If the interference is not irrelevant, fixing one inconsistency would affect the remaining one. Suppose we fix I_1 and I_2 in that order. We know that $\kappa_r(I_1) < \kappa_e(I_1)$, so we must choose reduction for I_1. This implies that the number of changes required for I_2 can never be increased by this process, because $A_r(I_1) \cap A_e(I_2) = \phi$. Thus, reduction will be the also the choice for I_2. We arrive to the same conclusion following the order I_2, I_1. Thus, the interference is irrelevant.

Condition b. Again, suppose we fix I_1 and I_2 in that order. We know that $\kappa_r(I_1) > \kappa_e(I_1)$, so we must choose expansion for I_1. This choice can never increase the number of changes that will be produced expanding I_2. Thus, I_2 will also be fixed by expansion. Moreover, the expansion path remains the same. Thus, the interference is irrelevant.

Condition c. If the order is I_1, I_2, and I_1 is corrected by expansion, the solution for I_2 is not changed because $A_e(I_1)$ is not in the area of interference. I_1 is corrected by reduction $A_r(I_2)$ and $A_e(I_2)$ remain unchanged. This is also true for the order I_2, I_1.

Condition d. If the order is I_1, I_2, and we correct I_1 by reduction, the nodes in $A_r(I_2)$ are not affected because $A_r(I_2) \notin A_i(I_1, I_2)$. If I_1 is fixed by expansion, the nodes in $A_r(I_2)$ are not affected because $T_1 \prec T_2$, and can only be expanded to $T_1.TO$, they are not modified in the interval of inconsistency of I_2. The same occurs if the order is I_2, I_1.

Proposition 4 (Inconsistencies of type ii). *Let I_1, I_2 be two inconsistencies of type ii, with intervals T_1 and T_2, respectively. Their interference is always irrelevant unless I_1 and I_2 are both overlappings with a common edge, such that the intersection between the time labels of all edges involved is not empty.*

Proposition 4 states that the only case when the two inconsistencies interfere in a relevant fashion is when, given three edges incident to a node (i.e., there is a common edge), $e_1(n_1, n, T_1), e_2(n_2, n, T_2), e_3(n_3, n, T_3)$, it holds that $T_1 \cap T_2 \neq \phi$, and $T_1 \cap T_3 \neq \phi$.

Proof. We have four possibilities: (1) I_1 and I_2 are gaps over a node n; (2) I_1 and I_2 are overlappings not involving a common edge; (3) there is a common edge (i.e., I_1 and I_2 involve just three edges); (4) I_1 is a gap and I_2 is an overlap.

Case (1). Let $lifespan(n_1) = [T_1, T_2] \cup [T_3, T_4] \cup [T_5, T_6]$, with $T_2 < T_3 - 1, T_4 < T_5 - 1$. Solving I_1 creates a new node n_{1c}, such that we will have

$lifespan(n_1) = [T_1, T_2]$, and $lifespan(n_{1c}) = [T_3, T_4] \cup [T_5, T_6]$. Clearly, fixing I_2 will only affect n_{1c}. The same occurs if we first fix I_2.

Case (2). Let $e_1(n_i, n_1, T_1), e_2(n_j, n_1, T_2), e_3(n_k, n_1, T_3), e_4(n_l, n_1, T_4)$ be edges such that $T_1 \cap T_2 \neq \phi \wedge T_3 \cap T_4 \neq \phi \wedge T_1 \cap T_2 \cap T_3 \cap T_4 = \phi$; also, $e_1 \neq e_2 \neq e_3 \neq e_4$. Fixing the first inconsistency, one of the two edges in the intersection interval. This, clearly, does not affect the remaining inconsistency, and the interference is irrelevant.

Case (3). Let $e_1(n_i, n_1, T_1), e_2(n_j, n_1, T_2), e_3(n_k, n_1, T_3)$, be edges such that $T_1 \cap T_2 \neq \phi \wedge T_2 \cap T_3 \neq \phi \wedge T_1 \cap T_3 = \phi$. If T_2 is reduced in one of the inconsistencies, the other one is not affected. As we did not assume any order, this happens when choosing the orders I_1, I_2 or I_2, I_1.

Case (4). It is clear that a gap and an overlap cannot occur during the same interval. If we first fix the gap (via node duplication), the overlap will remain in one of the nodes and will be fixed as if the gap never existed. If we, instead, fix the overlap first, the gap will not be affected. Thus, the interference is irrelevant.

Now we will address cycles (inconsistencies of type iii). In Section 4 we presented two solutions to the problem of fixing a cycle: (a) removing all edges in the cycle, which implies changing the lifespan of the nodes in the cycle, and may produce new inconsistencies of type i and ii, that will be fixed by reduction and node duplication, respectively. All the nodes affected belong to the reduction area of the inconsistency. Thus, in what follows we will denote this solution, *correction by reduction*, like in Section 4. Analogously, solution (b) (removing one edge in the cycle, if possible), potentially generates an inconsistency of type ii, and, as it was explained, an inconsistency of type i, which are corrected by expanding the intervals of one of the edges. Thus, all of the affected nodes are in the expansion area of the inconsistency, and we will also denote this solution *correction by expansion*.

Proposition 5 (Inconsistencies of type iii). *Let I_1, I_2 be two inconsistencies of type iii, with intervals T_1 and T_2, respectively. Their interference is irrelevant if at least one of the following holds:*

a. $\kappa_r(I_1) < \kappa_e(I_1) \wedge \kappa_r(I_2) < \kappa_e(I_2) \wedge A_e(I_1) \cup A_r(I_2) = A_e(I_2) \cup A_r(I_1) = \phi$
b. $\kappa_r(I_1) > \kappa_e(I_1) \wedge \kappa_r(I_2) > \kappa_e(I_2) \wedge A_e(I_1) \cup A_r(I_2) = A_e(I_2) \cup A_r(I_1) = \phi$
c. $A_i(I_1, I_2) = A_e(I_1) \cap A_r(I_2) \wedge T_1 \prec T_2$.
d. $A_r(I_1, I_2) = A_r(I_1) \cap A_r(I_2) \wedge T_1 \cap T_2 = \phi$.
e. *Let n_1 be the only node belonging to the cycle in I_1. Then,* $(A_e(I_2) \cap A_r(I_1) = n_1 \vee (A_e(I_2) \cap A_r(I_1) = \phi) \wedge (A_r(I_2) \cap A_e(I_1) = \phi \wedge T_1 \cap T_2 = \phi)$

Conditions (a) and (b) are analogous to the ones in Proposition 3, considering the definition of *correction by reduction* and *correction by expansion* for inconsistencies of type iii. Condition (e) means that the only node in the Area of Interference is a node belonging to I_1, is in the reduction area of I_2 but not in the expansion area of I_2, and the inconsistency intervals are disjoint.

Proof. (sketch) For conditions (a) and (b), the proofs are similar to Proposition 3. For condition (c) the proof is based on showing that, for instance, for the order I_1, I_2, reduction for solving I_1 does not affect the nodes in $A_r(I_2)$, because $A_r(I_1) \notin A_i(I_1, I_2)$. Expanding, instead, affects the nodes in $A_r(I_2)$, but there is no node added to or deleted from $A_r(I_2)$, because $T_1 \prec T_2$. We proceed analogously for the order I_2, I_1. The proof of condition (d) has a similar mechanism: expanding does not affect, because the expansion areas are not in the area of interference. Eliminating a cycle (reduction) of I_1 (I_2) affects the nodes in $A_r(I_2)$ ($A_r(I_1)$), but in different intervals (because $T_1 \cap T_2 = \phi$.) The idea is analogous for condition (e).

Proposition 6 (Inconsistencies of types i and ii). *Let I_1, I_2 be two inconsistencies of types i and ii, respectively, with intervals T_1 and T_2. Their interference is irrelevant if one of the following holds:*

    a. *I_2 is in the reduction area of I_1, and I_2 is not an overlapping or $T_2 \cap T_1 = \phi$.*
    b. *If I_2 is a gap, it occurs on a node in the expansion area of I_1 (i.e., $A_i(I_1, I_2) = A_{inf}(I_2)$), and $T_2 \cap T_1 = \phi$.*

Proposition 7 (Inconsistencies of types i and iii). *Let I_1, I_2 be two inconsistencies of types i and iii, respectively, with intervals T_1 and T_2. Their interference is irrelevant if one of the following holds:*

    a. *The number of changes needed for performing correction by reduction of I_1 and I_2 is less than the number of changes needed for performing correction by expansion over the same inconsistencies, and their areas of expansion and reduction have an empty intersection.*
    b. *The number of changes needed for performing correction by expansion of I_1 and I_2 is less than the number of changes needed for performing correction by reduction over the same inconsistencies, and their areas of expansion and reduction have empty intersection.*
    c. *If there is n in I_1 belonging to $A_r(I_2)$, then $T_1 \cap T_2 = \phi$.*
    d. *If there is n in I_2 belonging to $A_e(I_1)$, then $T_1 \cap T_2 = \phi$.*

Proposition 8 (Inconsistencies of types ii and iii). *Let I_1, I_2 be two inconsistencies of types i and iii, respectively, with intervals T_1 and T_2. Their interference is irrelevant if I_1 is a gap, and the node where it occurs is not in the expansion path of I_2.*

6   Conclusion

We have studied the problem of validating a set of temporal constraints in a temporal XML document, based in the data model presented in [12]. We proposed methods for checking the presence of inconsistencies in a document, and fixing them. We studied individual and combined inconsistencies, and state a set of conditions that make irrelevant the interference between them (i.e., each one can be treated and fixed independently from any other one). These conditions can be incorporated into algorithms for efficiently performing the fixing procedure.

This work can be a good starting point for studying and reasoning about temporal constraints with indeterminate dates, of the types presented in [6,9].

Acknowledgements. This work was supported by the Millennium Nucleus Center for Web Research, Grant P04-67-F, Mideplan, Chile.

References

1. T. Amagasa, M. Yoshikawa, and S. Uemura. A temporal data model for XML documents. In *Proceedings of DEXA Conference*, pages 334–344, 2000.
2. A. Balmin, Y. Papakonstantinou, and V. Vianu. Incremental validation of xml documents. *ACM Transactions on Database Systems*, 29(4):710–751, 2004.
3. D. Barbosa, A.O. Mendelzon, L. Libkin, L. Mignet, and M. Arenas. Efficient incremental validation of XML documents. In *ICDE*, pages 671–682, 2004.
4. S. Chawathe, S. Abiteboul, and J. Widom. Managing historical semistructured data. In *Theory and Practice of Object Systems, Vol 5(3)*, pages 143–162, 1999.
5. S. Chien, V. Tsotras, and C. Zaniolo. Efficient management of multiversion documents by object referencing. In *Proceedings of the 27th International Conference on Very Large Data Bases*, pages 291–300, Rome, Italy, 2001.
6. C. Dyreson and R. Snodgrass. Supporting valid-time indeterminacy. *ACM Transactions on Database Systems*, 23(1):1–57, 1998.
7. C.E. Dyreson. Observing transaction-time semantics with TTXPath. In *Proceedings of WISE 2001*, pages 193–202, 2001.
8. C. Gao and R. Snodgrass. Syntax, semantics and query evaluation in the τXQuery temporal XML query language. *Time Center Technical Report TR-72*, 2003.
9. F. Grandi and F. Mandreoli. Effective representation and efficient management of indeterminate dates. In *TIME'01*, pages 164–169, 2001.
10. B. Kane, H. Su, and E. Rundensteiner. Consistently updating XML documents using incremental constraint check queries. In *WIDM*, pages 1–8, 2002.
11. A. Marian, S. Abiteboul, G. Cobena, and L. Mignet. Change-centric management of versions in an XML warehouse. In *Proceedings of the 27th VLDB Conference*, pages 581–590, Rome, Italy, 2001.
12. A.O. Mendelzon, F. Rizzolo, and A. Vaisman. Indexing temporal XML documents. In *Proceedings of the 30th International Conference on Very Large Databases*, pages 216–227, Toronto, Canada, 2004.
13. B Oliboni, E. Quintarelli, and L. Tanca. Temporal aspects of semistructured data. *Proceedings of the Eight International Symposium of Temporal Representation and Reasoning*, pages 119–127, 2001.
14. Y. Papakonstantinou and V. Vianu. Incremental validation of XML documents. In *ICDT*, pages 47–63, 2003.
15. F. Rizzolo and A. Vaisman. Temporal XML documents: Model, index and implementation. *Submitted*, 2006.
16. F. Wang and C. Zaniolo. Temporal queries in xml document archives and web warehouses. In *Proceedings of the 10th International Symposium on Temporal Representation and Reasoning (TIME'03)*, pages 47–55, Cairns, Australia, 2003.

A Logic-Based Approach to Cache Answerability for XPath Queries

M. Franceschet[1,2] and E. Zimuel[1,2]

[1] Informatics Institute, University of Amsterdam,
Kruislaan 403 – 1098 SJ Amsterdam, The Netherlands
[2] Dipartimento di Scienze, Università "Gabriele D'Annunzio",
Viale Pindaro, 42 – 65127 Pescara, Italy

Abstract. We extend a recently proposed model checking-based algorithm for the evaluation of XPath queries with a cache strategy to store the results of the (most frequently) asked queries and to re-use them at occurrence. We experimentally show that, as soon as the cache is warm, the proposed optimization is quite effective. We complement our proposal with a broad experimental comparison of different strategies for XPath query processing.

1 Introduction

The XML Path Language version 1.0 (XPath, in the following), is a query language for XML documents proposed in 1999 by the World Wide Web Consortium(W3C) [1]. Compared to some later proposals of the W3C, like XPath 2.0 [2] and XQuery [3], the XPath language, and in particular its navigational fragment, or Core XPath [4], is simple, clean, and intuitive. As a result, XPath has become very popular among XML users and many software houses have extended their products with XPath tools. Moreover, researchers in both the computational logic and the database communities devised quite a large number of solutions for the evaluation of XPath queries, including tree traversal methods [4,5,6], model checking-based methods [7,8,9], automata-based methods [10,11,12], join-based methods [13,14,15], and sequence matching-based methods [16,17]. However, we are aware of few papers that aim to compare the relative performance of such algorithms ([18] compares join-based and sequence matching-based methods, while [19] evaluates XML indexes for structural joins).

This paper gives two contributions. We extend the above list of evaluation methods with a logic-based approach to answer XPath queries with the aid of cache mechanisms. Moreover, we make a thorough experimental comparison of the following four evaluation techniques for XPath:

TopXPath (Section 8.1 of [4]). The idea that lies behind this algorithm is to rewrite the original query into a Boolean combination of filter-free paths (sequences of steps without filters). The evaluation of the filter-free path is performed by reading the path string from left to right and sending the output of the current step to the input of the next step, if any. For instance, consider the query:

S. Amer-Yahia et al. (Eds.): XSym 2006, LNCS 4156, pp. 46–60, 2006.

$$\pi[\phi] = /\text{child} :: \text{site}/\text{child} :: \text{regions}[\text{descendant} :: \text{item}/\text{following} :: \text{payment}]$$

The method works in two phases. First, the query filter ϕ is rewritten by reading it from right to left and inverting each axis. The inverted filter becomes:

$$\varphi = \text{self} :: \text{payment}/\text{preceding} :: \text{item}/\text{ancestor} :: *$$

Then, the above query is evaluated as $\pi \cap \varphi$, that is, by taking the intersection of the result of π (with the singleton containing the tree root as initial context set) and the result of φ (with the set of all tree nodes as initial context set).

BottomXPath ([9]). The idea here is to rewrite the original query into a modal formula and then evaluate the formula *bottom-up*, that is, each formula is evaluated after the evaluation of its subformulas. As an example, consider again the above query $\pi[\phi]$. The corresponding modal formula is:

$$\text{regions} \wedge \langle\text{parent}\rangle(\text{site} \wedge \langle\text{parent}\rangle\text{root}) \wedge \langle\text{descendant}\rangle(\text{item} \wedge \langle\text{following}\rangle\text{payment})$$

where tags are interpreted as atomic propositions (root is a propostion that is true exactly at the tree root) and each axis is simulated by a corresponding modality. The modal formula is evaluated bottom-up exploiting the fact that the truth value of any subformula can be computed from the truth values of its direct subformulas.[1]

CacheBottomXPath. This is a cache optimization of BottomXPath that we propose and evaluate in this paper (see Section 2 for the details). The query is first converted into a modal formula and then chopped into a set of subformulas. Then, each subformula, in bottom-up order, is searched in the cache. If the subformula is found, no evaluation is performed, since the result has been already computed. Otherwise, the subformula is evaluated and its result is possibly stored in the cache.

Arb ([12]). This is an automata-based method. The XML document is first converted into a binary tree representation. Then, two deterministic binary tree automata, one working bottom-up and the other one working top-down, are generated from the query. The actual evaluation is performed in two steps: (i) first, the bottom-up query automaton runs on the XML binary tree; (ii) then, the top-down query automaton runs on the XML binary tree enriched with information computed during the bottom-up run. Finally, the entire XML document is returned with selected nodes marked up in XML fashion.

An analysis of the worst-case computational complexity of the above four methods does not help much to determine the most efficient evaluation strategy. Let us focus on the navigational part of XPath known as Core XPath [4], which is supported by all the above methods. Let k be the query complexity and n be

---

[1] This bottom-up principle holds for many modal and temporal logics. A notable example is Computation Tree Logic (CTL), a popular specification language in the context of formal verification of software and hardware systems [20].

the data complexity. On Core XPath, the worst-case complexity of TopXPath, BottomXPath, and CacheBottomXPath is $O(k \cdot n)$, while Arb terminates in $O(K + n)$, where K is an exponential function of k. A closer look inside the four algorithms reveals the following. In order to solve a query of length k on a tree of size n it happens that: (i) TopXPath visits each tree node a number of times between 0 and k (each node might be visited a different number of times) (ii) BottomXPath visits each tree node exactly k times; (iii) CacheBottomXPath visits each node the same number of times between 0 and k and it spends extra time proportional to the cache loading factor in order to search into the cache; and (iv) Arb visits each tree node twice (independently on the query complexity) and it spends extra time that might be exponential in k in order to build the tree automata. All the algorithms spend a constant amount of time at each node but BottomXPath (and its cache-based version) is particularly efficient since it operates mostly on Boolean values.

To have a better understanding of the relative performance of the methods under testing, we conducted a probing *experimental* evaluation on synthetic and simulated real data. The main goals of our investigation are: (i) to understand the effectiveness of the cache optimization introduced in CacheBottomXPath; (ii) to compare the performance of the top-down and bottom-up approaches implemented in TopXPath and BottomXPath, respectively, on randomly generated data, and (iii) to test the scalability of the automata-based method encoded in Arb when the query length grows. In particular, is the automata construction step a bottleneck for query processing in Arb?

The rest of the paper is as follows. In Section 2 we review BottomXPath and describe CacheBottomXPath. The results of our experimental evaluation are discussed in Section 3. We conclude in Section 4.

2   XPath Evaluation Methods

Even if the algorithms mentioned in Section 1 work on, or can be easily extended to, full XPath, we will evaluate them on the navigational fragment of XPath, or Core XPath, that was defined in [4]. With respect to full XPath, this fragment disallows the axes attribute and namespace, node tests different from a tag or *, comparison operators and functions. What remains can be used to navigate the XML tree only. The algorithms that we test essentially differ only on this fragment.

As noticed in [21], Core XPath can be viewed as a Modal Logic, interpreted over tree structures, whose modalities behave like the XPath axes. Modal Logic [22] extends Propositional Logic with modalities that, similarly to XPath axes, are used to browse the underlying relational structure. Let Σ be a set of proposition symbols. A *formula* in the multi-modal language is defined as follows:

$$\alpha = p \mid \alpha \wedge \alpha \mid \alpha \vee \alpha \mid \neg \alpha \mid \langle R_i \rangle \alpha$$

where $p \in \Sigma$ and $1 \leq i \leq c$ for some integer $c \geq 1$. A multi-modal logic for XPath contains a propositional symbol for each XML tag and a modality $\langle X \rangle$

for each XPath axis X. Modal formulas are interpreted at a given state of a given model in the usual way [22]. E.g., $\langle X \rangle \alpha$ is true at state s iff there exists a state t reachable from s through the relation X such that α is true at t. The *truth set* of a formula α w.r.t. a model M is the set of states of M at which α is true.[2]

We refer to [4] (Section 8.1) and [12], respectively, for a complete description of TopXPath and Arb. In the rest of this section, we review BottomXPath [9] and we introduce CacheBottomXPath. BottomXPath inputs an XML tree T and a Core XPath query q and returns the answer set for q with respect to T in the following two steps:

BottomXPath(T, q)
    1: translate q into a modal formula α_q;
    2: retrieve the truth set of α_q w.r.t. T;

The translation of step 1 works as follows. Each tag is mapped to a corresponding proposition symbol and * is mapped to the truth value true. Moreover, a new proposition root is introduced to identify the tree root. The query path is read from right to left and each axis (not belonging to a filter) is mapped to the modality corresponding to the inverse of the axis. Finally, each query filter is translated by reading it from left to right and by mapping each axis to the corresponding modality and each Boolean operator to the corresponding Boolean connective. For instance, the query:

/child::a[parent::b/following::c]/descendant::d[preceding::e or not(following::*)]

is mapped to the formula:

d $\wedge$ $\langle$ancestor$\rangle$(a $\wedge$ $\langle$parent$\rangle$root $\wedge$ $\langle$parent$\rangle$(b $\wedge$ $\langle$following$\rangle$c)) $\wedge$
($\langle$preceding$\rangle$e $\vee$ $\neg$$\langle$following$\rangle$true)

The truth set of the resulting modal formula (step 2 of BottomXPath) is computed by the procedure XPathCheck as follows. XPathCheck inputs an XML tree T and an XPath modal formula α and returns the truth set for each subformula of α (including α itself) in document order. The algorithm is similar to the model checking procedure for the temporal logic CTL, a popular specification language in the context of finite-state program verification [20]. We first describe the data structures used by the algorithm. XPathCheck takes advantage of a Boolean matrix A, where the rows represent formulas and the columns represent nodes, in order to label nodes with formulas that are true at them. Initially, each entry of A is set to 0. For each subformula of α numbered with i and each node of T numbered with j, the procedure sets $A[i, j]$ to 1 if and only if the formula i is true at the node j. Moreover, XPathCheck stores the tree T as a set of linked objects each of them representing a tree node. Each object contains a field with the preorder rank of the node, a field containing the XML tag of the element that the node represents, and pointers to the parent, first child, right and left siblings nodes. Finally, XPathCheck represents the formula

---

[2] In computational logic, the problem of finding the truth set of a formula is well-known as the (global) *model checking problem* [20].

α as its parse tree PT_α. Each node of PT_α represents a subformula β of α and it is stored as an object containing a field with the main operator of β, a field containing the index of the corresponding row in A, and pointers (at most 2) to the argument nodes of the main operator of β. It is convenient to insert in A the subformulas of α in postorder with respect to a visit of PT_α (so that the subformulas of α can be scanned bottom-up) and the nodes of T in preorder with respect to a visit of T (so that each truth set is sorted in document order).

XPathCheck works as follows. Given a tree T and a formula α, it processes each subformula β of α by visiting the parse tree PT_α in postorder. In this way, each subformula of β is checked before β itself is verified. The verification of β depends on the its main operator:

1. if β is root, then XPathCheck sets $A(\beta, 1)$ to 1 (the first column of A is associated to the tree root);
2. if β is *, then XPathCheck sets $A(\beta, j)$ to 1 for each node j;
3. if β is a tag a, then XPathCheck sets $A(\beta, j)$ to 1 for each node j tagged with a;
4. if β is $\beta_1 \wedge \beta_2$, then, for each node j, XPathCheck sets $A(\beta, j)$ to 1 if $A(\beta_1, j) = 1$ and $A(\beta_2, j) = 1$ (and similarly for the disjunction and negation cases)[3];
5. if β is $\langle X \rangle \beta_1$, then, for each node j, XPathCheck sets $A(\beta, j)$ to 1 if there exists a node k reachable from j trough the relation induced by X such that $A(\beta_1, k) = 1$.

The check of subformulas of the form $\langle X \rangle \beta_1$ depends on the axis X. In general, it is a tree searching algorithm that possibly labels nodes with $\langle X \rangle \beta_1$. For instance, if the axis is descendant, then the procedure first retrieves the nodes labelled with β_1 and then it labels each ancestor of such nodes with $\langle descendant \rangle \beta_1$ if the ancestor is not already labelled with it. Notice that, for each axis X, the formula $\langle X \rangle \beta_1$ can be checked by visiting each tree node only a constant number of times, hence in linear time with respect to the number of nodes of the tree. Moreover, most of the operations are performed on Boolean values. It follows that XPathCheck runs in time proportional to the product of the formula length and the XML tree size. Since the mapping from queries to formulas (step 1 of BottomXPath) takes linear time and the resulting formulas have linear lengths with respect to the lengths of the input queries, we can conclude that BottomXPath runs in $O(k \cdot n)$, where k is the query length and n is the XML tree size.

2.1   Cache Answerability for XPath Queries

BottomXPath repeats the computation of the truth set for each instance of the same subformula. This can be avoided as follows. Both a *formula cache M*,

---

[3] Notice that the matrix entries for β_1 and β_2 are known when β is processed, since β_1 and β_2 are subformulas of β and hence their postorder ranks in the parse tree are smaller than the postorder rank of β.

storing the past formulas, and a *truth set cache A*, storing the truth sets for past formulas, are maintained. When a new formula is checked, first the formula is searched in M. If the formula is found, then no further processing is necessary. Otherwise, the sub-formulas of the original formula that are not present in M are added to M and their truth sets are computed and added to A.

We now describe the optimization in more detail. Consider a formula α. We represent α with its parse tree PT_α and the truth set cache with a Boolean matrix A as described above. The new entry is the formula cache that is implemented using a *hash table M* where the keys are the formula strings and the collision resolution method is by chaining. Each object of the linked lists associated to the hash table contains the formula string, the index of the corresponding row in A, and the usual pointer to the next object in the list. The processing of α is as follows: (a) the parse tree PT_α is generated, (b) PT_α is visited in postorder and, for each node (subformula) x, the following steps are done:

1. the formula string s associated to x is built by visiting the tree rooted at x;
2. the string s is searched in the hash table M;
3. if an object y with key s is found in M, then x is updated with the row index of the matrix A corresponding to the formula s, which is read from y;
4. otherwise, a new row from A, say l, is assigned to the formula s, a new object for s is inserted in the hash table with the row index l, the object x is updated with the row index l, and finally the truth set for s is computed possibly updating the l-th row of A.

The described optimization is particularly effective in a client/server scenario. Consider the case of a static XML document on a server and a number of users ready to repeatedly query the document from remote clients. The server stores the query answer cache for all the posed queries, while each client stores the cache for the queries posed locally. It is possible for the same user to pose similar queries (containing common sub-queries) at different stages. Moreover, it is likely that different users ask for similar or even for the same query. When a query is posed on a client, first an answer for the query is searched in the local cache stored on the client. If the answer is found, then it is returned to the user. Otherwise, the sub-queries of the original query that do not have a cached answer are shipped to the server and the answers for them are searched in the global cache stored on the server. The found answers, if any, are shipped to the client user and the client cache is updated with them. The missing answers are computed on the server, the global cache on the server is updated with them, the answers are shipped to the client user and finally the client cache is also updated. When the querying is done, the query cache can be stored in secondary memory and loaded again if the querying restarts.

An important issue involved in the described optimization concerns the cache maintenance strategy [23]. Such a strategy specifies how to warm-up the cache, that is, how to populate the cache in advance with queries that are likely to be frequently asked. Moreover, it specifies when to insert new queries and to delete old ones from the cache. We did not implement any particular cache maintenance strategy in CacheBottomXPath. Indeed, our current goal is to compare high-level evaluation strategies for XPath. Such an evaluation might hint how to program an optimized full-fledged evaluator for XPath.

3   An Experimental Evaluation

This section contains the results of our experiments on both synthetic and simulated real data. We implemented TopXPath, BottomXPath, and CacheBottomXPath in C language, taking advantage of Expat XML document parser (`http://expat.sourceforge.net`). We used the Arb implementation that is available at Christoph Koch's website `http://www.infosys.uni-sb.de/ koch/ projects/arb`. We ran all the programs in main memory. We performed our experiments with XCheck [24], a benchmarking platform for XML query engines. We ran XCheck on an Intel(R) Xeon(TM) CPU 3.40GHz, with 2 GB of RAM, running Debian Gnu/Linux version 2.6.16. All times are in seconds (or fraction). Processing a query involves several steps, including parsing the document, compiling and processing the query, and serializing the results. The *response time* is the time to perform all these steps. We mostly measured the *query processing time* (the time spent for the pure execution of the query), which is the most significant for our purposes. Because of space limitations, this section contains only a fraction of the experiments and of the data analysis that we performed. The complete experimental evaluation is available at the website associated to this paper: `http://www.sci.unich.it/~francesc/pubs/xsym06`. The website includes also the source codes of the programs that we implemented for this paper. We stress that all the experiments that we performed are based on data (XML documents and queries) and software (query engines and data generators) that are publicly available and hence they are completely reproducible. We tried to devise experiments in the spirit of *scientific testing* as opposed to competitive testing [25], that is, experiments that allow to draw general conclusions instead of comparing absolute time values. In the rest of this section we will abbreviate TopXPath as TXP, BottomXPath as BXP, and CacheBottomXPath as CBXP.

3.1   Experiments on Synthetic Data

This section contains the results of our experiments on synthetic (i.e., artificial) data. Due to their flexibility, synthetic data are useful to uniformly test specific capabilities of an engine by using specific benchmarks (also known as microbenchmarks [26]). We evaluated the performance of the XPath engines under consideration while changing the following parameters: data size, data shape, query length, and query type.

We performed different experiments with different goals. An *experiment* consists of an input, and output and a goal. The experiment's *goal* is what we want to measure. The experiment's input is a set of XML documents (*data set*) and a set of XPath queries (*query set*). Finally, the experiment's output is a set of results that need to be interpreted with respect to the goal of the experiment. We generated the data set with MemBeR data generator [26]. It allows controlling different parameters for an XML document, including tree size, tree height, and maximum node fanout. As for the queries, they were generated with XPathGen, a random Core XPath query generator that we implemented for this paper.[4] XPathGen can generate queries with an arbitrary length and with an arbitrary nesting degree of filters. It allows controlling the following parameters for a query: length, axes probabilities, and filter probability. The query length is the number of atomic steps of the form axis::test that the query contains. Each axis has a corresponding probability of being selected during the query generation. This allows the generation of queries that are biased towards some of the axes. Finally, the filter probability controls the filter density in the query (that is, the number of query filters divided by the query length). This allows the generation of path-oriented queries (when the filter probability is low) and filter-oriented queries (when the filter probability is high). It is worth noticing that, in each generated query, each node test is * and the first step of the query is always descendant::*. As a consequence, it is very unlikely to generate queries with an empty result. Moreover, the intermediate and final results of the generated queries are quite large.

We used the documents described in the table below, where the meaning of the columns is as follows: n is the tree size (the number of tree nodes), avgd is the average node depth (the depth of a node is the length of the unique path for the node to the root), maxd is the maximum node depth (the height of the tree), avgf is the average node fanout (the fanout of a node is the number of children of the node), and maxf is the maximum node fanout.

doc	n	avgd	maxd	avgf	maxf	doc	n	avgd	maxd	avgf	maxf
D1	200,000	7.4	8	2.8	5	D5	500,000	12	13	2	61
D2	500,000	4	4	26	35	D6	50,000	6.7	7	4	9
D3	500,000	6.8	7	6	12	D7	5,000,000	6.9	7	8	16
D4	500,000	9.5	10	3	16	D8	100,000	6.8	8	4.6	5

We performed the following experiments:

Experiment E1. With this experiment we tested the engines' performance while increasing the filter probability. We set the query length $k = 10$ and varied the filter probability $p \in \{0, 0.25, 0.5, 0.75, 1\}$. Each axis is equi-probable. For each value of p, we generated 25 queries, ran them against document D1, and measured the overall query processing time. The results are below:

E1	$p = 0$	$p = 0.25$	$p = 0.5$	$p = 0.75$	$p = 1$
TXP	19.03	22.38	23.8	25.79	27.89
BXP	16.13	16.19	16.18	16.19	16.52
CBXP	10.28	8.97	8.51	8.68	10.03
Arb	15.41	14.47	13.96	14.19	14.31

Interestingly, TXP shows worse performance as the query filter density increases. This can be explained as follows. During query evaluation, TXP separates the

---

[4] The source code is available at the paper website.

query into paths and filters. Paths are evaluated form the tree root, while filters are processed with respect to the set of all tree nodes, which is more expensive. Hence, filter-oriented queries are more difficult for TXP. Independently on the filter probability, TXP is always the slowest while CBXP is always the fastest. Arb and BXP are competing.

Experiment E2. With this experiment we tested the engines' performance while increasing the query length. We set the filter probability $p = 0.25$ and varied the query length $k \in \{5, 10, 15, 20, 25\}$. All the axes are equi-probable. For each value of k, we generated 25 queries, ran them against document D1, and measured the overall query processing time. We also computed the query scalability factors.[5] The results are below (where the columns named qs contain the query scalability factors with respect to the adjacent query lengths):

E2	k = 5	qs	k = 10	qs	k = 15	qs	k = 20	qs	k = 25
TXP	13.65	0.82	22.31	0.94	31.57	0.85	35.95	1.09	48.87
BXP	9.42	0.86	16.25	0.88	21.5	1	28.07	1.03	36.09
CBXP	4.98	0.89	8.89	1.19	12.47	1.01	16.83	1.05	22.07
Arb	14.36	0.55	15.79	1.44	34.2	25.95	1183.41	5.52	8167.5

TXP, BXP and CBXP scale up linearly when the query length is increased. On the contrary, the performance of Arb is discontinuous, as witnessed by the query scalability factors. It is almost irrelevant to the query length up to length 10. However, for longer queries, the performance of Arb grows exponentially in the query length. This can be explained as follows. For long query strings, the time spent by Arb during the automata construction, which exponentially depends on the query length, dominates the pure query evaluation time (the time spent to run the automata), which is independent on the query length. CBXP shows the best global performance. BXP comes as second, while TXP and Arb competes up to length 15, where the performance of Arb explodes exponentially.

Experiment E3. With this experiment we tested the engines' performance while changing the document tree shape. We set the query length $k = 5$ and the filter probability $p = 0.25$. All the axes are equi-probable. We generated 25 queries according to these paremeters. As for the data set, we used documents in the sequence (D2, D3, D4, D5). All the document trees in the sequence have the same size and vary their shape. In particular, the trees in the sequence move from wide-and-short to narrow-and-long trees. For each document, we measured the overall query processing time. The results are below:

---

[5] Given a document D and two queries q_1 and q_2 of length l_1 and l_2 respectively, with $l_1 < l_2$, let t_1 be the processing time for q_1 on D and t_2 be the processing time for q_2 on D. The *query scalability factor*, as defined in [27], is the ratio $(l_1 \cdot t_2)/(l_2 \cdot t_1)$. If this factor is smaller than 1 (respectively, equal to 1, bigger than 1), then the engine scales up sub-linearly (respectively, linearly, super-linearly) when the query length increases.

E3	h = 4	h = 7	h = 10	h = 13
TXP	28.45	31.83	34.89	36.41
BXP	19.88	22.45	24.79	25.26
CBXP	10.3	12.11	13.65	13.39
Arb	38.42	38.37	37.74	30.4

Interestingly, TXP, BXP and CBXP perform better on wide-and-short trees, while Arb gives its best on narrow-and-long trees. Recall that the natural data model for Arb is a binary tree (arbitrary trees are preprocessed and converted to binary trees). This might explain why Arb is fastest on structures that are close to binary trees. Notice that document D5, on which Arb shows the best performance, has an average fanout of 2. As for global performance, CBXP is still the fastest. BXP comes as second, while TXP and Arb competes, with Arb outperforming TXP on narrow document trees.

Experiment E4. With this experiment we tested the engines' performance while increasing the document tree size. We set the query length $k = 5$ and the filter probability $p = 0.25$. All the axes are equi-probable. We generated 25 queries according to these paremeters. As for the data set, we used the sequence (D6, D3, D7) of documents of increasing size and width. Each document in the sequence has the same maximum depth and roughly the same average node depth. For each document, we measured the overall query processing time. We also computed the data scalability factors.[6] The results are below (where the columns named ds contain the data scalability factors with respect to the adjacent document sizes):

E4	n = 50,000	ds	n = 500,000	ds	n = 5,000,000
TXP	3.1	0.93	28.71	0.97	278.8
BXP	2.16	0.96	20.73	0.97	202.06
CBXP	1.22	0.95	11.62	0.98	113.58
Arb	4.28	0.65	27.69	1.06	293.01

Mostly, the scalability of all engines is linear. The sub-linear behavior of Arb in the first track depends on the time taken to build the tree automata, which is independent on the tree size. This time is dominated by the pure query processing time (the time to run the tree automata) in the second track. As for global performance, CBXP is still the fastest. BXP comes as second, while TXP and Arb are close.

Experiment E5. With this experiment we tested the engines' performance while changing the axes permitted in the queries. We set the query length $k = 5$, the filter probability $p = 0.25$, and varied the set of allowed axes as follows: (a) all the axes, (b) all the axes but following and preceding, (c) all the vertical axes (i.e., child, parent, descendant, ancestor), (d) all the forward vertical axes (i.e.,

---

[6] The *data scalability factor* is defined as for the query scalability factor except for the fact that it uses the size of the XML tree instead of the length of the query.

child and descendant). In each case, we generated 50 queries, ran them against document D3, and measured the overall query processing time. The results are below:

E5	(a)	(b)	(c)	(d)
TXP	56.33	38.8	37.1	39.86
BXP	40.48	28.35	28.77	29.12
CBXP	18.07	10.07	9.74	7.45
Arb	63.7	46.4	46.33	51.32

The message is clear: for all the engines under testing, following and preceding axes are the most expensive ones (compare columns (a) and (b)). If we prohibit these axes, the response time is almost the half. On the contrary, horizontal axes following-sibling and preceding-sibling are not problematic (compare columns (b) and (c)). The same for backward vertical axes parent and ancestor (compare columns (c) and (d)). In any case, CBXP is still the fastest, followed by BXP, TXP and Arb in this order.

Experiment E6. With this experiment we tested the performance of the cache optimization introduced in CBXP. We fixed the cache size to 64. We allowed all axes with the same probability and generated 500 queries by randomly choosing, for each query, a value for the query length $k \in \{1, 2, \ldots 10\}$ and for the filter probability $p \in [0, 1]$. We ran the queries against document D8. The results are illustrated in Figure 1. The left plot shows the processing times of the different engines for all the 500 queries. The right plot sums the processing times on adjacent intervals of 100 queries. In both plots, from top to bottom, Arb corresponds to the first (pink) line, TXP to the second (red) line, BXP to the third (green) line, and CBXP to the fourth (blue) line.

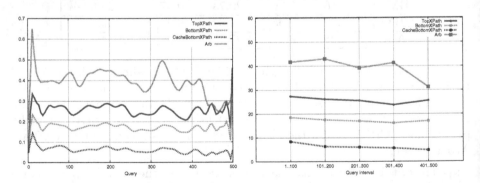

Fig. 1. The effectiveness of the cache

As for the effectiveness of the cache optimization, notice that CBXP is almost 3 times faster than BXP and, as expected, its relative performance increases as more queries are processed. Indeed, the ratios between the processing times of BXP and CBXP are 2.21, 2.78, 2.83, 2.89, and 3.56 on the 5 consecutive query intervals containing 100 queries, and the ratio is 2.77 on the whole query interval. As for global performance, CBXP is followed by BXP, TXP, and Arb in this order. If we set to 1 the time spent by CBXP, then the time consumed by BXP is 2.77, that of TXP is 4.02, and that of Arb is 6.3.

3.2   Experiments on Simulated Real Data

This section contains the results of our experiments on simulated real data. We generated the documents using XMark data generator XMLGen [28]. It generates scalable XML documents simulating an Internet auction website. We generated three documents of increasing size, that we named SmallDoc, MedDoc, and BigDoc. The table below contains the documents' characteristics, where s is the document size in MB (notice that the maximum fanout of the documents is quite different while the average fanout and the depths are constant):

doc	n	s	avgd	maxd	avgf	maxf
SmallDoc	167,864	11.1	4.55	11	3.66	2,550
MedDoc	832,910	55.32	4.55	11	3.66	12,750
BigDoc	1,666,310	111.12	4.55	11	3.67	25,500

As for the query set, we used a fragment of the XPath benchmark XPath-Mark [27]. Our benchmark consists of 11 queries, each focusing on a different axis, with a natural interpretation with respect to XMark documents. For instance, query Q4 asks for the American items sold in the auction and corresponds the the XPath query /child::site/child::regions/child::*/child::item[parent::namerica or parent::samerica]. See the paper website for the full list of queries.

The query processing time spent by each engine to execute the entire benchmark on the three documents is shown in following table. The columns named ds contain the data scalability factor for the adjacent documents:

Engine	SmallDoc	ds	MedDoc	ds	BigDoc
TXP	0.73	1.01	3.66	0.99	7.28
BXP	1.29	1.02	6.50	0.99	12.93
CBXP	0.72	1.00	3.58	1.00	7.18
Arb	80.84	1.01	404.92	0.93	750.08

TXP and CBXP are the fastest, followed by BXP. Arb is far behind. Hence, in this case, TXP outperforms BXP. The situation was the opposite on synthetic data. This behavior is interesting. While the evaluation strategy encoded in TXP is query-driven, that is, it tries to access only those nodes that will be eventually selected by the query, BXP, CBXP, and Arb strategies are blind in this respect and might visit nodes that will not be part of the solution. XPathMark queries are very selective, that is, their partial and final results are small compared to the document tree size. On the contrary, synthetic queries have large intermediate and final results (almost all the tree nodes are always in these sets). Hence, TXP has a big advantage on selective queries with respect to BXP and Arb. Nevertheless, exploiting the cache optimization, CBXP still competes with TXP on selective queries. An additional cause for the bad performance of Arb on this benchmark is the shape of XMark documents, which tend to have a large maximum fanout, while the natural data model for Arb is a binary tree. Finally, the data scalability of all engines is essentially linear.

The query processing and response times for each query in the benchmark with respect to MedDoc are depicted in Figure 2. For each query, from left to right, TXP corresponds to the first (red) bar, BXP to the second (green) bar, CBXP to the third (blue) bar, and Arb to the fourth (pink) bar. The relative performance on the other two documents is much similar.

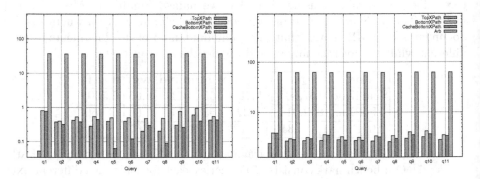

Fig. 2. Query processing (left) and response (right) times on MedDoc (log scale)

Moreover, the table below shows, for each engine, the minimum (min), maximum (max), average (mean), and standard deviation (deviation) of the processing times of the benchmark queries with respect to MedDoc. The ratio between the standard deviation and the mean is given in the last column (stability). This value is an indicator of the stability of the query response times for an engine.

engine	min	max	mean	deviation	stability
TXP	0.05	0.60	0.37	0.15	41%
BXP	0.40	0.95	0.53	0.17	32%
CBXP	0.06	0.77	0.32	0.20	62%
Arb	36.25	37.37	36.80	0.40	1%

The analysis per query confirms the above hypothesis about the performance of TXP and BXP. While TXP neatly outperforms BXP on highly selective queries like Q1, the performance of the two is comparable on queries with less selectivity like Q2. As expected, Arb is the most stable and TXP is less stable than BXP. CBXP is unstable due to the cold cache. We conjecture that CBXP is very stable if the cache is warm (well populated).

Finally, the effectiveness of the cache is well illustrated in Figure 3. The left plot refers to BXP and the right one is for CBXP. Notice how the cache optimization smooths the peaks of BXP. This action is more effective as the cache warms up.

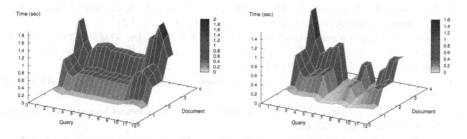

Fig. 3. The effectiveness of the cache in 3D

4   Conclusion

As mentioned in the introduction, many evaluation methods for XPath have been proposed. However, few attempts have been made to compare the performance of these methods. In particular, to the best of out knowledge, this is the first paper that empirically compares top-down and bottom-up methods for XPath. Our general conclusions are the following:

1. The cache optimization is effective and should be definitely integrated in an optimized full-fledged XPath/XQuery evaluator. Of course, a cache maintenance strategy should be adopted.
2. The top-down approach of TopXPath is more efficient than the bottom-up approach of BottomXPath on queries with high selectivity, while the opposite is true on poorly selective queries. Natural queries, like XPathMark ones, tend to be quite selective.
3. The tree automata-based approach implemented in Arb does not scale up with respect to the query length. When the query is relatively small, the approach is efficient and in fact the response times are independent on the query length, as claimed in [12]. However, this does not hold anymore when the size of the query grows.

References

1. World Wide Web Consortium: XML Path Language (XPath) Version 1.0. http://www.w3.org/TR/xpath (1999)
2. World Wide Web Consortium: XML Path Language (XPath) Version 2.0. http://www.w3.org/TR/xpath20 (2005)
3. World Wide Web Consortium: XQuery 1.0: An XML Query Language. http://www.w3.org/TR/xquery (2005)
4. Gottlob, G., Koch, C., Pichler, R.: Efficient algorithms for processing XPath queries. In: VLDB. (2002) 95–106
5. Gottlob, G., Koch, C., Pichler, R.: XPath query evaluation: Improving time and space efficiency. In: ICDE. (2003) 379–390
6. Gottlob, G., Koch, C., Pichler, R.: Efficient algorithms for processing XPath queries. ACM Transactions on Database Systems **30** (2005) 444–491

7. Afanasiev, L., Franceschet, M., de Rijke, M., Marx, M.: CTL model checking for processing simple XPath queries. In: TIME. (2004) 117–124
8. Hartel, P.: A trace semantics for positive Core XPath. In: TIME. (2005) 103–112
9. Franceschet, M., Zimuel, E.: Modal logic and navigational XPath: an experimental comparison. In: M4M. (2005) 156–172
10. Neven, F.: Automata theory for XML researchers. SIGMOD Record 31 (2002) 39–46
11. Neven, F., Schwentick, T.: Query automata over finite trees. Theoretical Computer Science 275 (2002) 633–674
12. Koch, C.: Efficient processing of expressive node-selecting queries on XML data in secondary storage: A tree automata-based approach. In: VLDB. (2003) 249–260
13. Al-Khalifa, S., Jagadish, H.V., Koudas, N., Patel, J.M., Srivastava, D., Wu, Y.: Structural joins: A primitive for efficient XML query pattern matching. In: ICDE. (2002) 141–152
14. Bruno, N., Koudas, N., Srivastava, D.: Holistic twig joins: optimal XML pattern matching. In: SIGMOD Conference. (2002) 310–321
15. Grust, T.: Accelerating XPath location steps. In: SIGMOD Conference. (2002) 109–120
16. Fan, W., Park, S., Wang, H., Yu, P.S.: ViST: A dynamic index method for querying XML data by tree structures. In: SIGMOD Conference. (2003) 110–121
17. Moon, B., Rao, P.: PRIX: Indexing and querying XML using Prüfer sequences. In: ICDE. (2004) 288–300
18. Moro, M.M., Tsotras, V.J., Vagena, Z.: Tree-pattern queries on a lightweight XML processor. In: VLDB. (2005) 205–216
19. Chen, C., Hsu, W., Li, H., Lee, M.L.: An evaluation of XML indexes for structural join. SIGMOD Record 33 (2004) 28–33
20. Clarke, E.M., Grumberg, O., Peled, D.A.: Model Checking. The MIT Press (1999)
21. Marx, M.: Conditional XPath, the first order complete XPath dialect. In: PODS. (2004) 13–22
22. Blackburn, P., de Rijke, M., Venema, Y.: Modal Logic. Cambridge University Press (2001)
23. Hsu, W., Lee, M.L., Yang, L.H.: Efficient mining of XML query patterns for caching. In: VLDB. (2003) 69–80
24. Afanasiev, L., Franceschet, M., Marx, M., Zimuel, E.: XCheck: A platform for benchmarking XQuery engines (demonstration). In: VLDB. (2006) http://ilps.science.uva.nl/Resources/XCheck.
25. Hooker, J.N.: Testing heuristics: We have it all wrong. Journal of Heuristics 1 (1996) 33–42
26. Afanasiev, L., Manolescu, I., Michiels, P.: MemBeR: a micro-benchmark repository for XQuery. In: XSym. Volume 3671 of LNCS. (2005) 144–161
27. Franceschet, M.: XPathMark: an XPath benchmark for XMark generated data. In: XSym. Volume 3671 of LNCS. (2005) 129–143 http://www.science.uva.nl/~francesc/xpathmark.
28. Schmidt, A., Waas, F., Kersten, M.L., Carey, M.J., Manolescu, I., Busse, R.: XMark: A benchmark for XML data management. In: VLDB. (2002) 974–985 http://www.xml-benchmark.org.

FLUX: Content and Structure Matching of XPath Queries with Range Predicates*

Hua-Gang Li, S. Alireza Aghili, Divyakant Agrawal, and Amr El Abbadi

University of California at Santa Barbara
{huagang, aghili, agrawal, amr}@cs.ucsb.edu

Abstract. Range queries seek the objects residing in a constrained region of the data space. An XML range query may impose predicates on the numerical or textual contents of the elements and/or their respective path structures. In order to handle content and structure range queries efficiently, an XML query processing engine needs to incorporate effective indexing and summarization techniques to efficiently partition the XML document and locate the results. In this paper, we describe a dynamic summarization and indexing method, FLUX, based on Bloom filters and B^+-trees to tackle these problems. We present the results of extensive experimental evaluations which indicate the efficiency of the proposed technique.

1 Introduction

XML has gained wide acceptance as an emerging standard and is being employed as a key technology for data exchange, integration and storage of semi-structured data. The XML data model, due to its rich presentation (content and semi-structuredness), poses unique challenges to effectively support complex queries. Powerful and flexible query capabilities have been developed [1, 2, 6, 8, 13, 17–19, 21, 23] to extract structural patterns from XML documents. These techniques are mainly based on the structural join by using some encodings on XML document elements. Queries on such ordered XML trees often impose predicates on the content of ELEMENT *labels* (keyword search) and/or their corresponding *structural relationships* (structural pattern search). These queries require the presence of some keywords in the document tree along with the conformation of the keyword instances with some structural patterns, which might be a specific linear path structure or a subtree/twig structure in the underlying data. For instance, Q = /dblp//article/[2004 ≤ year ≤ 2005] represents such a query with a linear path structure, which matches all the journal articles published between year 2004 and 2005 from the dblp [15] bibliography database. In addition, approximate top-k matching of XML queries were studied in [20].

XML query languages [7, 11] provide support for *content-and-structure* (CAS) class of queries. Additionally, full-text keyword search techniques [5] have been added to XML query languages to support more sophisticated full-text content retrieval. Furthermore, the XQuery and XPath query languages provide support

---

* This research was supported by the NSF under IIS-0223022 and CNF-0423336.

S. Amer-Yahia et al. (Eds.): XSym 2006, LNCS 4156, pp. 61–76, 2006.

for queries with *range predicates* which are also one of the fundamental function-
alities supported by general database query processing engines. In this paper,
the class of content-and-structure (CAS) single path queries are extended to include (*i*) *range* predicates over content, as well as (*ii*) *structure* predicates and,
furthermore, efficient techniques are proposed for processing them. We refer to
them as *XPath range* queries.

The efficient evaluation of such XPath range queries is determined by the
choice of an efficient execution and data access plan which is one of the critical responsibilities of the database optimizer. For instance, consider a possible
query plan for Q where the query engine has to perform the XPath range query Q'
= /dblp//article/[year = 2004 OR year = 2005] to find all the journal articles
published in the year 2004 or 2005. The dblp dataset contains 111,609 instances
of the [/article/year] path structure and only 259 instances of [/year/2005].
That is the [year = 2005] predicate will return 259 instances while the structure predicate [/dblp//article /year] results in 111,609 instances. Hence, it is
essential to utilize the *selectivity*[1] of the structural elements for efficient evaluation of the XPath range queries. An efficient query execution plan should apply
the evaluation starting at the more selective segments of the query. However, one
of the main challenges involved in such execution plans for XPath range queries
is that range predicates, which happen to be more selective in this case, typically
involve the leaf level of the XML document tree. Moreover, pushing the evaluation down to the leaves of the tree should be accompanied with the appropriate
leaf indexing techniques to avoid inspecting a large number of leaf nodes. It is
clear that plans such as Q' do not utilize the common optimization technique of
pushing down the selection operation down to the leaves of the query plan tree.
Ignoring the selectivity of the path elements results in the exponential growth of
the intermediate result set which must be retrieved from the database. We argue
that it is essential to utilize effective summarization and indexing techniques to
reduce the search space based on the content and most *selective* elements of the
XML document collections.

In this paper, we develop an XML query processing system for XPath range
queries named FLUX. FLUX employs an efficient B$^+$-tree based index structure
to locate the leaf matches to the range predicate of a query in its initial stage.
Each leaf match, n_i, of the document tree stores a *compact path signature* of the
root-to-leaf path structure ending at n_i, using the notion of Bloom filter [4]. In
the next step, the path signatures of each matched leaf instance n_i is compared
with the query's path signature to eliminate those instances whose path signatures are very different from that of the query. To the best of our knowledge, this
is the first attempt to specifically address the matching of XPath queries with
range predicates in XML document collections. The main features of FLUX are
summarized as follows:

- An efficient B$^+$-tree based indexing scheme is constructed on the *indexable*
  (e.g., textual, numerical, date, etc.) elements/attributes of the XML document for effective retrieval and matching of the query's range predicate.

---

[1] The fraction of the structural elements that satisfy the predicate.

- FLUX incorporates a novel bit-wise hashing scheme based on the notion of Bloom filter on ELEMENT and ATTRIBUTE contents of XML document trees. A family of hash functions are applied on the path components where each path is summarized to a compact bit vector signature. As a result, the path matching can be performed very efficiently through the comparison of path signature bit vectors.
- Extensive experimental evaluations demonstrate the effectiveness of FLUX for XPath range queries on real and synthetic XML datasets.

The rest of the paper is organized as follows: Section 2 presents the problem definition. Sections 3 and 4 provide the descriptions of range and path matching procedures, respectively. Section 5 finalizes the FLUX algorithm followed by Section 6 which provides the experimental results and analysis. Section 7 concludes the work.

2   Problem Formulation

XML documents are rooted ordered tree structures where each node in the document tree corresponds to the document's ELEMENT, ATTRIBUTE, or TEXT nodes. The TEXT nodes represent the values of their parent ELEMENT nodes, and ATTRIBUTE nodes introduce branches of their parent ELEMENT nodes. In this paper, we focus on simple XPath Range expressions which are defined as follows:

Definition 1. (*XPath Range Expression*). *A simple XPath expression* $p = e_1 t_1 e_2 t_2 \ldots e_k R$ *is called an* XPath range expression *(XPR), where* e_i *denotes an Ancestor-Descendant (AD, //) or Parent-Child (PC, /) edge, and* t_i *denotes the tag of an* ELEMENT *or* ATTRIBUTE, *and* R *represents a range predicate (sentinel) over an indexable element/attribute (e.g., numerical, textual, date, etc.), respectively.*

Example 1. $q_1 = $ /dblp//article/[2004 $\leq$ year $\leq$ 2005], and $q_2 = $ /management/ /employee/[90K $\leq$ salary $\leq$ 100K] represent XPR expressions on dblp and an employee database, respectively. For instance, in q_1: $e_1 = $ /, $t_1 = $ dblp, $e_2 = $ //, $t_2 = $ article, $e_3 = $ /, and $R = $ [2004 $\leq$ year $\leq$ 2005].

Definition 2. (*Path Signature*). *Assume that* $p = e_1 t_1 e_2 t_2 \ldots e_k t_k$ *is an XPath expression, where* t_k *is an indexable element/attribute, and* HF *is a family of hash functions, which map each tag of* p *onto a set of hash values. The hash values of the tags* $(t_1, t_2, \ldots, t_k)$ *are collectively combined[2] to construct a single bit-vector signature for the path structure* p.

Given an XML dataset and an XPath range expression, we need to locate and retrieve all the qualifying matching instances. Matching the query against an XPR instance of the dataset involves comparing their corresponding path structures and evaluating the range predicate over the instance. The range predicate match

---

[2] Details are discussed in Section 3. Intuitively speaking, it is to use these hash values to set the bits in a bit-vector.

of the sentinel R of the query expression seeks all the corresponding instances in the database having sentinel r such that $r \in R$. For instance, considering the query q_1 (from Example 1), this phase corresponds to locating all the instances of the *year* attribute being in the range of [2004, 2005], which are referred to as *range-matched* instances. Furthermore, the path structure signatures of all the range-matched instances are compared against the query's path structure signature. If the path structure signature is close enough (similarity measurement as defined in Definition 3) to the query's path structure signature, the path structure will be further checked against the query's structure to determine whether it is an exact match to be finally reported as answer to the query.

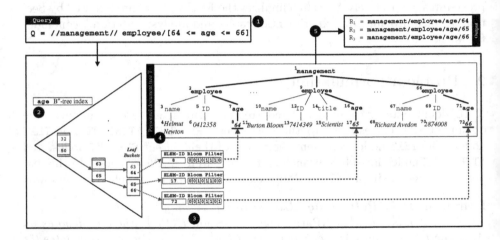

Fig. 1. FLUX Search model

Definition 3. (*Candidate Matching Instance*). *Given the XPR expression* $q = e_1 t_1 e_2 t_2 \dots e_t R$, *and any XPR range-matched instance* $p = e_1' t_1' e_2' t_2' \dots e_{t'}' r$ *of the database, let HF denote a family of hash functions which map a path structure onto a bit-vector. Moreover, let* $f{:}u \to 2^{\aleph}$ *denote a function on bit-vectors which returns the set of all indices of the "set" bits of any bit-vector* u. *Then, the XPR range-matched instance* p *is called a candidate matching instance to* q, *if*

$$f(\,HF(e_1 t_1 \dots e_t)\,) \subseteq f(\,HF(e_1' t_1' \dots e_{t'}')\,), and \ r \in R.$$

For instance, given two path structures q and p, where $HF(q) = 100001$ and $HF(p) = 101101$, then p is called a candidate matching instance of q because $f(HF(q)) = \{1, 6\} \subseteq f(HF(p)) = \{1, 3, 4, 6\}$.

Definition 4. (*Path & Range Components*). *An XPath range expression* $p = e_1 t_1 e_2 t_2 \dots e_k R$ *consists of two main components, a **path expression component** denoted by* $Q^\rho = e_1 t_1 e_2 t_2 \dots e_k$ *and a **range predicate (sentinel) component** $Q^\eta = R$.*

Example 2. The XPath range expression q_2 = /management//employee/[90K $\leq$ salary $\leq$ 100K] consists of two components: the *path expression component* Q^ρ = /management//employee/salary and the *range predicate component* Q^η = 90K $\leq$ salary $\leq$ 100K.

Given an XPR query Q, FLUX proceeds in two different phases, (i) finding the regions in the database satisfying the range predicate component Q^η of the query (**range matching**), and (ii) matching the query path component Q^ρ against the *range-matched* instances of the database (**path matching**). Range matching is the initial step and the results of this stage are passed to the path matching phase for structure matching and refinement of the answers. The following sections provide the details of the range and path matching procedures.

3   Range Matching

Any range query may benefit from efficient indexing mechanisms to quickly locate and retrieve the intersecting portions of the database satisfying the range predicate. Popular indexing techniques such as B$^+$-trees and R-trees have been extensively applied to alleviate such problems in the general context of range predicate queries. The *range matching phase* of FLUX employs an indexing technique based on B$^+$-trees on the *range predicate component* Q^η of the query for the effective reduction of the search space.

An offline procedure constructs a B$^+$-tree index on the *indexable elements/ attributes* (e.g, numerical, textual, date, ...) of the XML document. Part 2 in Figure 1 depicts a portion of one such index tree, constructed on the age element of a typical XML employee database. For instance, the last leaf bucket stores the age content information for two existing age values 65 and 66 in the database. Each instance (e.g. age = 66) also holds the bit-vector signature of the actual path component leading to this node (details provided in the next section), and its corresponding ELEM-ID information. The ELEM-ID is the *preorder traversal rank* of the corresponding node in the actual XML document. For instance, the node instance with age = 66 has preorder rank of 72, which is shown in the document tree of Figure 1, named as the node ^{72}66. Note that, each individual occurrence of an internal or leaf node has a unique preorder value.

It is important to note that our proposed encodings (as explained above) is different from the encoding schemes used in [1, 6, 11, 17]. Those encoding schemes associate interval/regional encoding with every node, based on the document order. For instance, each label may consist of (*start, end, level*) values for each node, acquired from the *preorder* traversal of the document, which is used to (i) help identify PC or AD relationships, and (ii) impose a logical document order among the nodes. We argue that, it is enough to use the preorder ranks of the nodes to impose the document order. Moreover, each node is associated with a parent pointer in order to locate its parent node. Given a leaf instance node n_i, the parent pointer $parent(n_i)$ is used to construct the complete leaf-to-root path originating from n_i. This complete path structure is constructed in the last stage of the path matching phase as the final round of path comparison.

4   Path Matching

Given an XPR query Q and the range-matched instances p_i of the database, the *path matching phase* performs the necessary steps to identify those path structure instances p_i whose path component p_i^ρ matches the path expression component Q^ρ. In the offline phase, each path expression of the database is hash-mapped and summarized by a compact bit-vector signature by collectively applying a family of hash functions on the element tags of each path based on the notion of Bloom filter [4]. In the following, we will introduce the Bloom filter and the motivations behind incorporating it.

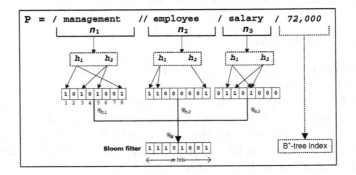

Fig. 2. A Bloom filter example

Bloom filter is a space-efficient data structure to probabilistically represent a set and its elements to support highly accurate *set membership* queries [4]. The Bloom filter B consists of a bit vector of length m, and a family of k independent hash functions. Given a set $S = \{n_1, n_2, \ldots, n_{|S|}\}$, a family of hash functions are used to construct a bit-vector signature for S. Figure 2 depicts the construction of a Bloom filter bit-vector signature using $k = 2$ independent $m = 8$-bit hash functions h_1 and h_2, on the path set $S = \{\texttt{management}, \texttt{employee}, \texttt{salary}\}$, where $n = |S| = 3$, from an employee database.

In general, given each element $n_i \in S$, the family of hash functions h_j ($1 \le j \le k$) are used to map n_i into a bit-vector. All the entries of the bit vector are initially set to zero. In order to construct the desired bloom bit-vector B_{n_i}, all the k hash functions h_j are applied to n_i. The application of each h_j on n_i results in "*setting*" some entries of B_{n_i} to 1. For instance in Figure 2, the application of hash function h_1 on n_1, $h_1(n_1 = \texttt{management})$ *sets* the 1st and 8th bits of the corresponding bit-vector B_{n_1}. Similarly, $h_2(\texttt{management})$ sets the 3rd and 5th bits of B_{n_1}. To construct the bloom bit-vector for the whole set $S = \{n_1, n_2, \ldots, n_{|S|}\}$, the resulting bit-vectors B_{n_i} are combined to form the bloom bit-vector B_S. The combination of the bit vectors B_{n_i} may be performed through a simple logical OR operation. That is, the bit vectors resulting from the application of h_1 and h_2 on the path element $\texttt{management}$, $\texttt{employee}$, and $\texttt{salary}$ of Figure 2, are combined using a logical OR function to construct the bloom bit-vector signature B_{P^ρ} ($=B_S$) for the path component P^ρ = /management//employee/salary. The ith entry of B_{P^ρ} is *set* to 1 if and only if the ith bit vector entry of at least one of the path components B_{n_1}, B_{n_2} or B_{n_3} has been set to 1. For instance, in Figure 2 the 8th-bit of the final Bloom filter B_S is *set* because the 8th-bit of B_{n_1} (or similarly B_{n_2}) is set. Note that, such application of Bloom filter relaxes the edge requirement as imposed by the query. This feature helps to additionally identify and report those instances whose path structure components are very similar to the query, yet having different edge structure.

Subsequently, to test whether the query's path component Q^ρ is similar to an instance path component B_{P^ρ} of the database, the same set of hash functions are applied to B_{Q^ρ} and all the corresponding bit-vector entries are *set* to 1. If all the "*set*" entries of B_{Q^ρ} match with their counterpart in B_{P^ρ} (that is $h(B_{Q^\rho}) \subseteq h(B_{P^\rho})$), it implies that the database path component B_{P^ρ} is identical to B_{Q^ρ} with some probability. The set of all such path structure instances is a superset of the actual (exactly-matched) answer set.

However, there is a chance of B_{P^ρ} and B_{Q^ρ} being identical while the actual path components P^ρ and Q^ρ are different (e.g. by-chance collisions/similarity of the "*set*" entries of Q^ρ and P^ρ). In such a case, a *filter error* (*false positive*) is said to have occurred. The performance of the hash functions of the Bloom filter depends on the *filter error ratio*, which is proven by B. H. Bloom [4] to be as follows. Let n be the number of nodes (or elements) in the set S (or path component P^ρ), m the size of the bit vector and k the total number of hash functions. The filter error ratio is defined as $\left(1 - e^{-\frac{kn}{m}}\right)^k$. For instance, the formula suggests a filter error of only 2.8% for $n = 3$, $m = 8$ and $k = 2$. Moreover, one of the most interesting features of the Bloom filter is that it guarantees not to incur any *false negatives* while being highly accurate and very space-efficient. Note that one of the shortcomings of this approach is the lack of support for updates. However, a variation of Bloom filter, *Counting Bloom Filter* [10], can be employed to resolve such a shortcoming.

Based on the above discussion, we can observe that the Bloom filter representation of each path structure provides an efficient mechanism to compare each path component of the document tree against their counterpart in the query. We next introduce the overall procedure of the FLUX algorithm which combines the features of range and path matching schemes.

5   FLUX Algorithm

Given the document tree T, the offline phase starts by performing a *preorder traversal* on T and assigns preorder ranks (ELEM-ID) to each node of T (the number on the top-left of each node in Figure 1). These preorder ranks create a virtual document order. FLUX consists of five individual phases as described in the following. Due to the space limit, we omit the algorithmic details of the FLUX procedure here.

1) Offline Index Creation. The FLUX offline manager constructs a B^+-tree index structure on the *indexable attributes* of the XML document collection (e.g. `age`, `salary`, `year`, and `date`). The leaves of each such B^+-tree store the attribute content (e.g., `age` value), ELEM-ID, and the bloom bit-vector signature of the root-to-leaf path structures of the corresponding nodes. For instance, the node corresponding to `age` = 64 at the leaf bucket level of B^+-tree of part 2 in Figure 1 stores the *preorder rank* ELEM-ID (e.g. 8 in this instance) of the actual node of the document tree whose `age` attribute has the value 64. Moreover, it stores the bloom bit-vector signature of the root-to-leaf path structure ending at that particular node. For instance, for the node `age` = 64 located at the B^+-tree leaf bucket of part 2 in Figure 1, the bit-vector 00101110 represents the bloom signature of the root-to-leaf path structure /management/employee/age of the node [8]64 of the document tree in part 4 of Figure 1, where the numbers 1,2 and 7 denote the ELEM-IDs of the element tag instances of `management`, `employee` and `age` element nodes, respectively.

2) Query Segmentation. This phase segments the query expression Q = //management//employee/[64≤age≤66] into the path component $Q^\rho = /$ /management//employee/age and the numerical predicate component $Q^\eta = [64 \leq \text{age} \leq 66]$.

3) Range Lookup. The search part of this phase corresponds to find the range-matched instances of the query range predicate (Lines 2-5 of the algorithm in the appendix shows such a procedure). For instance, the corresponding B^+-tree of the `age` range attribute is searched for potential candidate bucket nodes matching the predicate in Q^ρ (e.g. nodes 64, 65 and 66 in the part 2 of Figure 1 for [64 ≤ age ≤ 66]).

4) Path Matching and Filtration. Let $B_{p_1}, \ldots, B_{p_k}$ denote the bloom signatures of each of the k matches of the database (e.g., the Bloom filter of the path component /[1]management/[2]employee/[7]age which ends at node [8]64), whose contents have already been matched with the query's range predicate Q^η. This stage is responsible for matching the path component of the query B_{Q^ρ} against the path components of the range-matched instances $B_{p_1}, \ldots, B_{p_k}$. It ranks each matching instance B_{p_i} based on its similarity to B_{Q^ρ}. The path matching procedure corresponds to the invocation of the `BloomFiltration()` function at lines 14-15 of the algorithm described in the appendix where its definition is provided at lines 30-36. After filtering out the false positives, the `candidPath` holds the results of candidate matching instances to Q in the database. Finally, the actual path structures of the non-filtered matches are constructed (using the node pointers from leaf-to-root), compared against the query and reported to the user.

6   Experimental Evaluations

We implemented the FLUX system using *Java 1.4.2* and ran our experiments on a *Pentium M-2GHz* processor with *2GB* of main memory, using a page size of 1KB (determine the number of indexed data items which a leaf node can have and the number of key/pointers which an internal node can have for the B^+-tree.), cache size of 100KB, and LRU cache replacement policy. We compared our proposed technique with PathStack [6] which is the best in the literature for simple XPath queries. The PathStack technique is also implemented using *Java 1.4.2*. Two variations of PathStack were implemented in terms of the way of retrieving the XML document elements residing in the range specified in the query for the structural join: one variation uses B^+-tree index and the other variation does not. This is mainly because that we wanted to make sure that the advantage of using FLUX is not necessarily overshadowed by the indexing solution alone.

The experimental evaluations were performed on a set of both synthetic (XMark [24] containing information about an auction site) and real (dblp[3]) XML datasets. The dblp dataset (sized of 127MB) consists of 3,332,130 element nodes with an average and maximum depth of 2.9 and 6, respectively. We generated a set of synthetic XMark datasets with scaling factor ranging from 0.1 to 1.2 for the experimental evaluation. The average depth for the XMark datasets is 5. The number of hash functions used for constructing the Bloom filter is 4. For each element along the path which leads to an instance of the range attribute, its MD5 digest (a 128-bit cryptographic message) is computed [16]. This 128-bit message is evenly divided into 4 groups. Each 32-bit group is further transformed into an integer ranging from 0 to the Bloom filter size $-$ 1. Unless otherwise stated, the Bloom filter size was chosen to be 14 bits for dblp dataset and 16 bits for XMark datasets which will be explained later in this section.

The results presented in this section were generated by averaging the results from running a workload of 100 random queries on dblp and XMark datasets. The dblp query template was chosen as Q_D = /dblp/article/[$\$LB \leq$ year $\leq \$UB$], for different random values of $\$LB$ and $\$UB$. Similarly, the XMark query template was selected as Q_X = /regions//item//mail/[$\$LB \leq$ date $\leq \$UB$]. The range values [$\$LB$, $\$UB$] were chosen randomly from the <year> and <date> domain space in the year range 1945 to 2003 and date range 01/01/1998 to 12/28/2001. The dblp dataset includes 328,831 path instances leading to the year element, which is the reason behind using Q_D as the query template for dblp dataset since it provides a large candidate set. The richness of the path structure which leads to the <date> element is the reason behind choosing Q_X as the query template for XMark dataset (more structural variations on Q_X can be applied for the structural effect study). Moreover, different amount of random noise was imposed on the dblp and XMark datasets to create path structure variation at the element names. For instance, if $x\%$ noise is imposed on the dblp dataset and assume that there are N root-to-leaf paths leading to year element, then $N\times x\%$ of them will be modified by randomly changing one or more element tags to create the path structure variation. Following are some notations used in the upcoming figures:

---

[3] Acquired from the University of Washington's XML Data Repository accessible through *http://www.cs.washington.edu/research/xmldatasets/*

• **Total Candidates:** Number of all the possible year instances (dblp) and date instances (XMark) in the database for the inspected range resulting from the range query search on the B^+-tree index structure lookup phase.

• **Remaining Tuples:** The number of candidates left for further inspection after pruning the intermediate results by comparing their Bloom filter signature against the Bloom filter signatures of the query.

• **Actual Answers:** The number of actual answers in the database to the query.

• **False Positive Rate (FPR):** The FPR is calculated as $(RemainingTuples - ActualAnswers)/RemainingTuples$, which indicates how close the filtration gets to the actual answer set.

Figures 3-6 analyze the effect of *range length*, *Bloom filter size*, the imposed *noise*, and the *scalability analysis* on the **Filtration**, **False Positive Rate (FPR)** and **Response Time** effectiveness of FLUX, on the dblp and XMark datasets, respectively.

6.1 Effect of Range Length

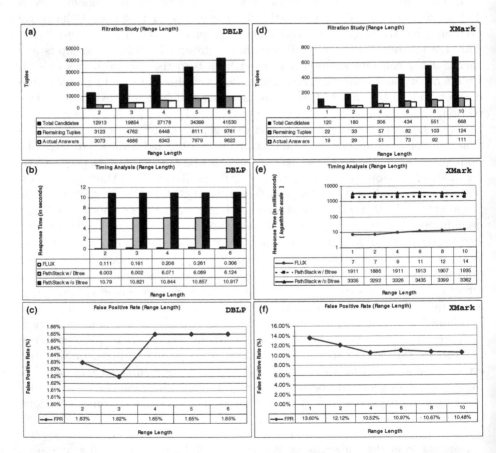

Fig. 3. Effect of range length variation on the filtration, FPR and response time

Figure 3 depicts the effect of the range length $r = |\$UB - \$LB|$ on the performance of FLUX on dblp and XMark (scaling factor = 1, size ≈ 113MB and noise = 30%) datasets. The query's range length/extent is varied from 2 (narrow) to 6 (moderately wide), and 1 (narrow) to 10 (wide) on the dblp[4] and XMark datasets, respectively. FLUX succeeds in pruning a substantial fraction of the candidate result set in the Bloom filter comparison phase as we can observe from Figure 3(a) and 3(d). For instance, in Figure 3(a), the column pertaining to $r = 3$ indicates that the application of bloom filtration reduces the number of total candidates from 19854 tuples to 4762 tuples, or in other words, to 24% of the total candidate result set. Figures 3(b) and 3(e) depict the total response time of performing the designated operations, as a function of range length compared with PathStack [6] (with and without using B$^+$-tree index structure). The running time of FLUX consistently outperforms PathStack on both dblp and XMark datasets. For instance, in Figure 3(e) FLUX performs 100-times faster on average when compared to PathStack (with B$^+$-tree index structure). Figures 3(c) and 3(f) depict the stability of False Positive Rate (FPR), which stays within 2% of the remaining tuples as the range length varies for dblp dataset and 14% for the XMark dataset.

6.2   Effect of Bloom Filter Size

Figure 4 analyzes the effect of Bloom filter size (in *bits*) as it varies from 10 to 20 bits and 6 to 20 bits on dblp and XMark datasets. The XMark dataset of this section was generated with a scaling factor of 1, with about 113MB in size and 30% imposed noise at the path element names. Figures 4(a) and 4(d) validate the intuitive expectation that the larger choice of the bloom signature length should result in more effective filtration. Figures 4(b) and 4(e) depict the response time analysis of FLUX when varying the bloom bit-vector size in answering the same set of 100 random queries on each respective dataset. The filtration (Figures 4(a) and 4(d)) and response time (Figures 4(b) and 4(e)) performance of FLUX improves consistently as the size of the bloom bit-vector increases from 10 to 14 bits for the dblp dataset and 10 to 16 bits for the XMark dataset. This is due to the fact that, the chance of bloom signature collision[5] reduces as the size of the bloom signatures increases. When the bloom bit-vector increases from 14 to 20 for the dblp dataset and 16 to 20 for the XMark dataset, the filtration effectiveness still increases while the query response time does not due to the fact that larger size of Bloom filter will incur more time to retrieve the corresponding data. Hence, we choose 14 bits for the dblp dataset and 16 bits for the XMark datasets for constructing Bloom filters in a timely manner. Moreover, Figures 4(c) and 4(f) demonstrate the filtration effectiveness of FLUX which is shown in the reduction of FPR when increasing the size of Bloom filter.

---

[4] e.g. 1999 ≤ /year ≤ 2003 has the range extent of $r = |2003 - 1999| = 4$.
[5] The probability bloom hash functions assign an identical bloom signature to two different path structures.

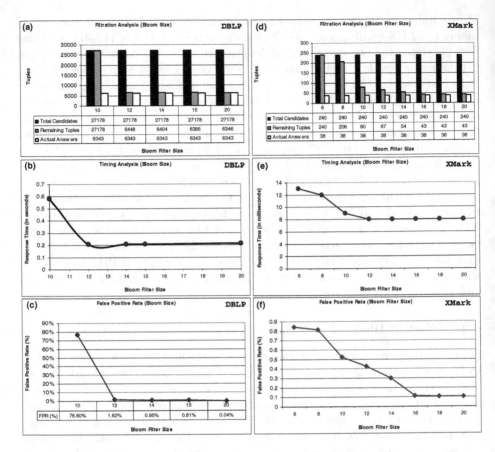

Fig. 4. Effect of the size of Bloom filter signature (in *bits*) on filtration, FPR, and response time

6.3 Effect of Noise in Data

For this set of experiments, we introduced random noise at the element names, varying from 1% to 5% on dblp dataset and 1% to 8% on XMark dataset, respectively. Figure 5 depicts the effect of the imposed noise ratio on the overall performance of FLUX. As expected, the introduction of more noise results in larger FPR as shown in Figures 5(c) and 5(f). However, despite the introduction of noise, FLUX performs very efficiently in filtration ratio and response time as observed in Figures 5(a) and 5(d), and Figures 5(b) and 5(e), respectively. FLUX substantially outperforms PathStack regardless of the amount of noise imposed on the data as shown in Figures 5(b) and 5(e). Relative to PathStack, FLUX performs even better when more noise is inherent in the dataset, which is a very desirable feature when the query is posed on datasets with variations in their representation or not necessarily conforming to a unified schema or Document Type Definition (DTD).

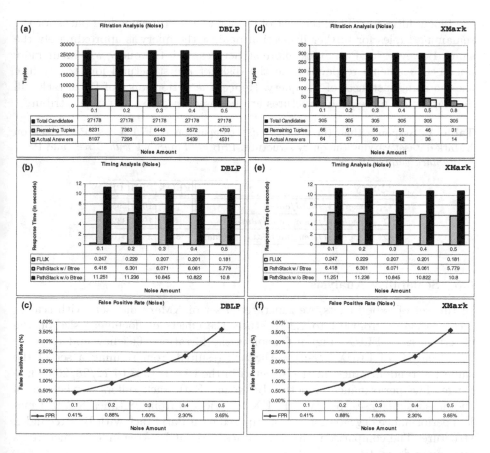

Fig. 5. The results of applying random noise with various intensity on the element names

6.4   Query Structure Variation

Table 1 depicts the response time analysis when varying the query structure in FLUX and PathStack (with and without B$^+$-tree index). From type Q_1 to Q_3, more element tags are imposed on top of the range attribute to create more complex path structures. The results were acquired by averaging the running time of 100 random range queries of type Q_i (of Table 1). The range domain was selected in the 01/01/1998 to 12/28/2001 date range and each random range query has length 4. The Bloom filter size was selected to be 16 bits. The incorporated XMark dataset was generated using a scaling factor of 1 with 30% noise. In all the observed cases, FLUX consistently outperformed PathStack. The performance of FLUX is slightly affected when the path structure of the query tends to get more complicated due to the bottom-up computation approach. The set of the remaining tuples for each type of query is the same after using the bloom filtration. Thus the cost of retrieving the corresponding paths for the remaining tuples for further inspection against the query is approximately the same. However, for PathStack, more structures with the query will incur more document elements retrieved from the disk for the structural join to produce the matching instances of the query. Hence, the performance of PathStack will decrease when more path structures are imposed on the same range attribute.

Table 1. Response time (in *milliseconds*) comparison of FLUX v.s. PathStack on XMark dataset varying the query structure. PSB = *"PathStack with Btree"* and PS = *"PathStack without Btree"*.

Query	FLUX	PSB	PS
$Q_1 = regions//mail/date$	7.9	1521	2937
$Q_2 = regions//item//mail/date$	8	1901	3323
$Q_3 = regions//item/mailbox/mail/date$	8.1	2307	3708

6.5   Scalability Analysis

In this set of experiments, we generated a set of XMark datasets with scaling factors ranging from 0.1 to 1.2 to study the effects of document size on the effectiveness of FLUX. Figure 6 depicts the filtration efficiency and response time analysis of FLUX versus PathStack resulted from running a set of the same 100 random range queries selected in the 01/01/1998 to 12/28/2001 date range. The performance of both FLUX and PathStack suffers as the size of the dataset increases, however, FLUX experiences from 98 times to 215 times less performance degradation rate compared with PathStack with B^+-tree index structure. The comparison with PathStack without B^+-tree index structure, is even more dramatic.

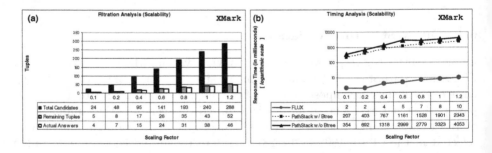

Fig. 6. The scalability analysis on XMark datasets

7   Conclusion

This paper proposed an efficient technique, named FLUX, for answering complex range queries in a database of XML documents. FLUX incorporated a B^+-tree based index structure on the contents of range attributes. It uses the notion of Bloom filters to associate a structure signature to each range attribute instance. The filtration performed by the bloom signatures of FLUX reduced the search space to a minor fraction of the intermediate result set. Experimental results demonstrate that the filtration, response time, false positive rate, speedup and scalability of FLUX consistently outperforms PathStack [6] on both real and synthetic datasets. The FLUX procedure proceeds with range matching followed by path matching. Nevertheless, depending on the selectivities of both the range and the path structure, it might be preferable to apply the structure matching first and then the range matching, or vice versa. Part of our future research work will include adapting FLUX or designing new index structures to handle the cases with selective structures.

References

1. S. Al-Khalifa, H.V. Jagadish, J.M. Patel, Y. Wu, N. Koudas and D. Srivastava, Structural Joins: A Primitive for Efficient XML Query Pattern Matching. ICDE, 141–152 (2002).
2. S. Al-Khalifa et al., Querying Structured Text in an XML Database. SIGMOD, 4–15 (2003).
3. S. Amer-Yahia, L.V.S. Lakshmanan and S. Pandit, FleXPath: Flexible Structure and Full-Text Querying for XML. SIGMOD, 83–94 (2004).
4. B.H. Bloom, Space/Time Trade-offs in Hash Coding with Allowable Errors. Communications of the ACM **13(7)**, 422–426 (1970).
5. C. Botev, J. Shanmugasundaram and S. Amer-Yahia, A TeXQuery-Based XML Full-Text Search Engine. SIGMOD, 943–944 (2004).
6. N. Bruno, N. Koudas and D. Srivastava, Holistic twig joins: optimal XML pattern matching. SIGMOD, 310–321 (2002).
7. D. Chamberlin, Daniela Florescu, Jonathan Robie, Jérôme Siméon and Mugur Stefanescu, XQuery: A Query Language for XML. W3C Working Draft, http://www.w3.org/TR/xquery (2001).
8. S. Chien, Z. Vagena, D. Zhang, V.J. Tsotras and C. Zaniolo, Efficient Structural Joins on Indexed XML Documents. VLDB, 263–274 (2002).
9. CiteSeer Scientific Literature Digital Library and Search Engine, http://citeseer.ist.psu.edu
10. L. Fan, P. Cao, J.M. Almeida and A.Z. Broder, Summary Cache: A Scalable Wide-Area Web Cache Sharing Protocol. SIGCOMM, 254–265 (1998).
11. T. Grust, Accelerating XPath location steps. SIGMOD, 109–120 (2002).
12. L. Guo, J. Shanmugasundaram, K.S. Beyer and E.J. Shekita, Efficient Inverted Lists and Query Algorithms for Structured Value Ranking in Update-Intensive Relational Databases. ICDE, (2005).
13. H. Jiang, W. Wang, H. Lu and J. Xu Yu, Holistic Twig Joins on Indexed XML Documents. VLDB, 273–284 (2003).
14. R. Kaushik, P. Shenoy, P. Bohannon and E. Gudes, Exploiting Local Similarity for Indexing Paths in Graph-Structured Data. ICDE, 129–140 (2002).
15. DBLP Bibliography Server, http://dblp.uni-trier.de/
16. Alfred J. Menezes, Paul C. van Oorschot, and Scott A. Vanstone. Handbook of Applied Cryptography. CRC Press, 1997 (.)

17. Q. Li and B. Moon, Indexing and Querying XML Data for Regular Path Expressions. VLDB, 361–370 (2001).
18. J. Lu, T. Chen and T.W. Ling, Efficient Processing of XML Twig Patterns with Parent Child Edges: A Look-ahead Approach. CIKM, 533–542 (2004).
19. J. Lu, T.W. Ling, C.Y. Chan and T. Chen, From Region Encoding to Extended Dewey: On Efficient Processing of XML Twig Pattern Matching. VLDB, 193–204 (2005).
20. A. Marian, S. Amer-Yahia, N. Koudas and D. Srivastava, Adaptive Processing of Top-K Queries in XML. ICDE, (2005).
21. P. Rao, B. Moon, PRIX: Indexing And Querying XML Using Prüfer Sequences. ICDE, 288–300 (2004).
22. F. Weigel, H. Meuss, K.U. Schulz and F. Bry, Content and Structure in Indexing and Ranking XML. WebDB, 67–72 (2004).
23. H. Wang, S. Park, W. Fan and P.S. Yu, ViST: A Dynamic Index Method for Querying XML Data by Tree Structures. SIGMOD, 110–121 (2003).
24. A. R. Schmidt et al., The XML Benchmark Project. Technical Report INS-R0103, CWI (2001).

A Resource Efficient Hybrid Data Structure for Twig Queries

John Wilson, Richard Gourlay, Robert Japp, and Mathias Neumüller

Department of Computer and Information Sciences
University of Strathclyde, Glasgow, UK
{jnw, rsg, rpj, mathias}@cis.strath.ac.uk

Abstract. Designing data structures for use in mobile devices requires attention on optimising data volumes with associated benefits for data transmission, storage space and battery use. For semistructured data, tree summarisation techniques can be used to reduce the volume of structured elements while dictionary compression can efficiently deal with value-based predicates. This paper introduces an integration of the two approaches using numbering schemes to connect the separate elements, the key strength of this hybrid technique is that both structural and value predicates can be resolved in one graph, while further allowing for compression of the resulting data structure. Performance measures that show advantages of using this hybrid structure are presented, together with an analysis of query resolution using a number of different index granularities. As the current trend is towards the requirement for working with larger semi-structured data sets this work allows for the utilisation of these data sets whilst reducing both the bandwidth and storage space necessary.

1 Introduction

Recently the memory, battery power and processor capabilities of mobile devices have increased greatly, but despite these advances the memory available to the system remains a critical resource for data-intensive mobile applications. Increasingly, mobile services rely on XML for the storage and transmission of data. Care needs to be taken in the representation of such data to support optimal processing. Indexing can be achieved by external data structures although the original XML needs to be retained to validate queries. Conceptually XML can be represented as a graph with vertices used to indicate data items and structural interrelationships shown by arcs. The structural elements can be compressed by retaining only a skeleton representation of the graph and dictionaries can be used to support non-redundant storage of leaf values.

Here we describe a hybrid system that uses signatures as an exchange mechanism for combining both of these approaches to produce an optimally efficient representation of XML data. The motivation for the model is outlined in the next section. Section 3 describes the components of the data structure and the benchmark queries used. The results of varying parameters on query performance are

S. Amer-Yahia et al. (Eds.): XSym 2006, LNCS 4156, pp. 77–91, 2006.

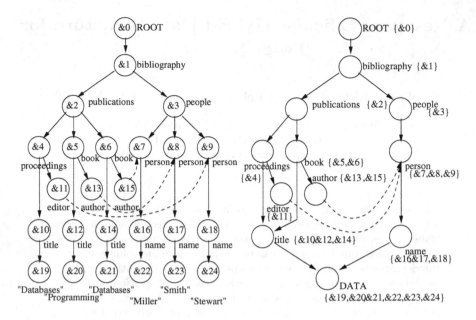

Fig. 1. Example source   **Fig. 2.** (2,0)-F+B-index

given followed by a discussion of the meaning that these results have for the data model presented. We show that different combinations of vertices can be used to help the resolution of queries involving both structural and value predicates. Grouping based on path similarity is useful when resolving structural aspects of a query but leaf values are needed to resolve queries on atomic value predicates.

1.1   Motivation

XML is a representation of semistructured data that is widely used in distributed, Internet-based applications. Tags can be used to represent the labeling and the edges are indicated by the hierarchical structure. Arbitrary graphs can be encoded in this flat-file representation through the use of special ID:IDREF pairs.

Queries over XML typically include both structural and value predicates. Query 1 provides an example that seeks to return the authors of books with the title 'Databases'. Figure 1 shows the data graph of the example source with vertex identifiers added to each node.

Query 1 (Books on Databases) *//book[/author & /title/DATA='Databases']*

Since Query 1 contains only forward facing query axes, it can always be answered by a single traversal of the data structure. However, this technique becomes impractical for very large data instances. For that reason, index structures are employed by most DBMS.

The structural index approach is illustrated by the work of Kaushik et al. [20,18]. Bisimilarity (i.e. the sharing of common subtrees) allows resolution of path location steps in linear time [4]. A family of indexes $((j,k)$-F+B-index) can be constructed using a range of values for forward or backward bisimilarity. Excluding the path from the root vertex, the longest forward facing path in the query graph has length two (book/title/DATA). There are no backward directed paths so the (2,0)-F+B-index shown in Figure 2 is the smallest covering index for the structural part of the example query.

Embedding the structural part of Query 1 into the index graph of Figure 2 can be done using the same algorithm that could be used to embed it into the data graph (since the graphs are bisimilar). The complexity of the embedding process remains unchanged but the size of the graph has been reduced from 25 vertices in Figure 1 to twelve vertices in Figure 2. Such a reduction in size can be expected for most semistructured data sources, as most practical data graphs contain only very few structural building blocks [3]. The structural elements of the query can be resolved against the index graph but the original data graph needs to be maintained in order to resolve the value predicate.

The query evaluation process, starting with the atomic value predicate is presented in terms a dictionary-based structure (DDOM [28]). Figure 3 shows the fully indexed dictionaries and the structural array of a part of the example source. Using this approach on Query 1 the existence of title vertices containing the atomic value 'Databases' can be quickly verified. These are the entries at the addresses **8** and **24** in the structural array, corresponding to the vertices &19 and &21 of Figure 1. Equally the index on the tag name dictionary can be used to verify that there exist book and author vertices in the data graph. A linear scan through the structural array is needed to verify ancestor-descendant relationships between entries. In the example given, a scan for the first book entry starting at position **11** leads to a title entry at address **15**, but none of the identified atomic value entries is encountered before the closing tags of the title and book entries are found at positions **17** and **18** respectively. Thus this entry, corresponding to vertex &5 of the data graph, does not represent a valid result. The similar scan starting at the book entry at position **19** matches all the required entries from the list of potential descendants, thus the result is valid.

Storing the complete range using the start and end addresses of the sub-tree rooted by a node as shown in Figure 3, allows derivation of the ancestor-descendant relationship using this information alone. The fact that identifiers can be used to indirectly encode structural relationships between nodes of a tree will be used by the hybrid representation presented here. Although this allows the validation of the structural constraints between individual nodes, it still does not allow the selection of a set of nodes based on their structural properties as can be achieved using the index graphs.

Where data is distributed across a number of hosts, local caching can be a useful tool for improving query response times. To maximize the benefit of this kind of approach, it is important to optimize cache utilization by the application. This is helped by making the data representation as compact as possible to improve the possibility of a query being resolved on the cache. Where the cache is found to be inconsistent, it is again important that refreshing is

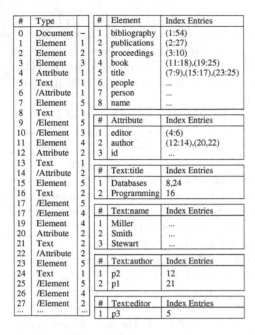

#	Type	
0	Document	–
1	Element	1
2	Element	2
3	Element	3
4	Attribute	1
5	Text	1
6	/Attribute	1
7	Element	5
8	Text	1
9	/Element	5
10	/Element	3
11	Element	4
12	Attribute	2
13	Text	1
14	/Attribute	2
15	Element	5
16	Text	2
17	/Element	5
17	/Element	4
19	Element	4
20	Attribute	2
21	Text	2
22	/Attribute	2
23	Element	5
24	Text	1
25	/Element	5
26	/Element	4
27	/Element	2
...	...	...

#	Element	Index Entries
1	bibliography	(1:54)
2	publications	(2:27)
3	proceedings	(3:10)
4	book	(11:18),(19:25)
5	title	(7:9),(15:17),(23:25)
6	people	...
7	person	...
8	name	...

#	Attribute	Index Entries
1	editor	(4:6)
2	author	(12:14),(20,22)
3	id	...

#	Text:title	Index Entries
1	Databases	8,24
2	Programming	16

#	Text:name	Index Entries
1	Miller	...
2	Smith	...
3	Stewart	...

#	Text:author	Index Entries
1	p2	12
2	p1	21

#	Text:editor	Index Entries
1	p3	5

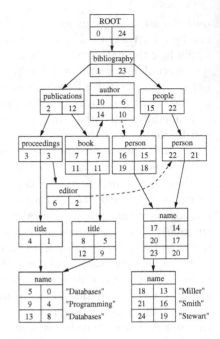

Fig. 3. Structure array and indexed domain dictionaries used by DDOM

Fig. 4. Combination of structural index with signature information

carried out with optimum efficiency. Whilst the F+Bindex approach provides a fast and compact index for resolving queries on XML by supporting the structural part of query resolution, validation ultimately requires access to the native data representation. The DDOM approach replaces the native representation with a more compact structure that exploits the redundancy often occurring in large data structures. The purpose of the hybrid structure is to combine the benefits of an F+Bindex with the benefits of the DDOM representation. The intention is to produce a data structure that has the fast response characteristics of the former whilst removing the need to refer to the original data structure.

2   The Hybrid Approach

The approaches described in Section 1.1 originate from different perspectives and lack a common element that could be used for their combination. Index graphs allow set-at-a-time operation and maintain structural relationships between vertex-sets whilst abstracting away from the individual vertices of the data graph. Dictionary compression organises data into homogeneous domains and maintains the identity of individual vertices of the data graph but their structural relationships are not exposed directly. The approach investigated here is based on signatures as an exchange mechanism between the index graph and signature representation approaches. A signature is a compact representation of an important property of a given source and in this paper it is used to describe the structural relationships between tree nodes. Two schemes are presented that can be used to label the node-set of an ordered tree. The definitions can be equally applied to unordered trees, where an arbitrary ordering of the child nodes will suffice. The target domain of these labellings is the set of natural numbers, thus they will be called *numbering schemes* in order to distinguish them from arbitrary labelling schemes. The numbering scheme implies an order on the node-set given by the order of the natural numbers identifying them, even if the data model is considered to be that of an unordered tree.

2.1 Related Work

Numbering schemes can be used to provide a basis for connecting structural indexes with value representations. Dietz [13] describes a data structure for efficient presentation of trees based on linked lists. An application of this structure is the determination of the ancestor-descendant relationship based on the pre and post-order numbering schemes. Grust [16] analysed the numbering scheme further and identified that the original pre- and post-order numbering scheme can also be used to answer queries along the previous/following axis of XPath. The scheme was extended to include direct references to parent nodes and type information (attribute node type or tag name and element) which allows for the storage of the complete XML document in a single relation. Additional work has been carried out on the use of numbering schemes in the context of XML to improve efficiency [33,23,11], implement join processing [3], deterministic addressing [21] and relational database containment [34].

Several methods of efficiently compressing XML data have been developed, the earliest XML conscious compressors took advantage of context based compression to reduce the data size from text based compressors. Cheney [8,9] shows a scheme that can achieve 10–25% reduction from even most efficient text based compressors, while these schemes reduce the size of the data there is no way to query directly this structure, the data must first be fully decompressed before being able to query the data. The next broad range of XML compressors are data structures which build on XMILL [24] to allow the analysis and storage of the data into a queryable form [30,10,2,26], these allow efficient path queries over the data while still needing large parts to be decompressed in the worst cases. We have already investigated the use of dictionary compression techniques for representing XML data structures [28] and other investigators have also examined the decomposition of XML into array-based structures [12]. Ferragina et al [14] developed a data structure combining several benefits of simple zip compression with fast access by linking two compressed array structures.

Early work on different kinds of index structures for semi-structured data focused on query optimisation for the Lore system [25]. The main thrust of this work was the development of heuristics that determine when to use each of the four specific forms of indices (value, text, link and path index) provided by their experimental base. Halverson et al [17] identify the need to combine pattern matching techniques based on inverted lists with the navigational approach typical for XML tree traversal algorithms pointing out the lack of integration between these two lines of research. They provide a cost model for query answering in each of these domains, identifying query classes that are better suited to either approach or to a combination of both. Full path indexing can be supplemented by dynamic indexing that responds to query load [7]. Sub-graphs and feature extraction can also be used as the basis of index construction [32,35]. Indexing techniques for supporting cross-border queries in mobile applications are also emerging [22].

Vectorization of XML, developed by Choi and Buneman [12,5] combines the XMill [24] approach for compact representation of atomic data with the approach for skeleton compression by sharing subtrees [4] to address XML join queries. Their fundamental assumption is that the skeleton of typical XML documents is small and thus can be kept in memory. The actual data is only used in the last stage of their join algorithm, avoiding unnecessary I/O operations.

Kaushik et al [19] extend their original work [18,20] on structural indices for path expressions to include keyword constraints on the contained atomic data. They propose a general strategy to combine structural indices with inverted lists in order to address this class of queries efficiently and test their approach using the Niagara system [27]. As their value indices are based on techniques developed in the context of information retrieval systems, their resulting query system includes support for finding the k most relevant results. An efficient structure for disk-based implementation of the F&B-index has been developed by Wang et al [31]. Structural and index values are combined by Amato et al [1] by extending the structure to incorporate the values for some elements or by incorporating B^+−Tree value indexes within the structure. Even within unstructured data there are often regular substructures that allows for a mapping to semi or fully structured data, Buneman et al [6] describes such a mapping to an edge-labelled graph structure.

2.2   Contribution

The fundamental difference between the work reviewed and that presented here lies in the integration of the different index structures. In the scheme of Kaushik et al, the inverted list structure uses signature entries based on the same numbering scheme proposed here, extended by an identifying label of the corresponding index node in the structural index. The approach presented here breaks the atomic data dictionaries according to the structural groupings. These groupings replace the use of inverted lists. Consequently the part of the dictionary corresponding to a structural grouping can be incorporated into the node of the index graph representing it. By doing this the secondary data structure of the index graph becomes a primary data structure that replaces the original data graph rather than summarises it.

The data grouping implied by the DDOM approach is based on local backward-bisimilarity with $k_b = 1$. Thus a structural index graph based on vertex bisimilarity with $k_b = 1$ can be combined with the indexed dictionaries presented in Figure 3. At the same time, the vertex identifiers used in both the dictionaries and the index graph can be replaced with the entries based on Dietz' numbering scheme, creating a unique address space for validation purposes. The approach suggested here can be seen as the cross-product of an index graph with a signature with its leaf nodes being replaced by domain dictionaries. Figure 4 illustrates this using the (1,1)-F+B-index graph of the example data graph shown in Figure 1. In this illustration, the incorporated atomic value dictionaries are suppressed in order to simplify the diagram.

3   Experimental System

The purpose of the experimental work is to compare query performance on the data graph structure with performance on the hybrid NSGraph. In addition, it seeks to characterise the optimal granularity in the NSGraph structure. To carry this out, thirteen queries representing five query classes were executed against the datagraph and NSGraphs with forward and backward bisimilarity ranging from 0 to 3. Xmark [29] data sets ranging from 1 MB to 30 MB were used in this experimental work. Branching path expressions are used as a basic query language since they represent an important subset of the expressive power of selective query languages for semistructured data. Only the edges in the tree view of the data graph are considered, i.e. additional graph arcs are not supported. As a consequence of this restriction to trees, the query language can also be restricted to allow tree patterns only, thus eliminating the need for backward directed axes. The semantics of query expressions are restricted to return the matches of the root predicate of the query tree, rather than the matches of an arbitrary predicate. The resulting language allows the encoding of tree patterns, thus its expressions are called *tree* or *twig pattern expressions* [33,3].

3.1   Data Structure Components

The data structure is based on index graphs utilising the concept of local bisimilarity and is referred to as an NSGraph, In addition, a variant of Dietz' numbering scheme annotated by node level information [3,13] and a dictionary structure such as that used in DDOM is also needed. The choice of the family of index graphs developed by Kaushik et al. is based on their clearly described and mathematically sound model. The complete F&B-index is the minimal covering index graph for all branching path expressions.

The prototype allows for the complete family of indices based on local bisimilarity so that the influence of different data groupings on the query performance can be investigated. The concept of bisimilarity generalises this approach by grouping vertices by their label first and then refining this organisation based on incoming or outgoing paths. The possibility for parameterising the bisimulation results in different refinements of the dictionary structure to be tested. An important special case will be the $(k, 1)$-F+B-index, which combines the properties of the $F(k)$-index for structural constraints with the previously used atomic value dictionaries grouped by parent nodes.

Class	Query	Tree pattern	Results
K	K1	//item[/description/keyword/DATA="*attires*"]	5
	K2	//open-auction[/bidder/date/DATA="*1999*"]	1997
	K3	//person[/profile/education/DATA="*Graduate*"]	463
	K4	//closed-auction[/annotation/happiness/DATA="*10*"]	276
Q1	Q1a	//person[/name/DATA="Klemens Pelz" & /watches & /emailaddress& /creditcard]	0
	Q1b	//person[/name/DATA="Klemens Pelz" & /watches & /emailaddress & /phone]	0
Q2	Q2a	//profile[/income & /education & /gender]	972
	Q2b	//profile[/income & /education & /gender/DATA="male"]	477
	Q2c	//profile[/income & /education & /gender/DATA="female"]	495
Q3	Q3a	//item[/location/DATA="United States" & /payment/DATA="*Creditcard*"& /quantity/DATA="1"]	2044
	Q3b	//item[/payment[/DATA="*Creditcard*" & /DATA="*Cash*"]]	1540
Q4	Q4a	//description[//text[//keyword & /bold]]	4579
	Q4b	//description[//text/*[/keyword & /bold]]	109

Fig. 5. The benchmark tree pattern queries in BPE syntax

3.2   The Benchmark Queries

The tree pattern queries collected for this experiment (Figure 5) are designed to highlight the response of the implemented query algorithms to a number of distinct challenges within the designated query class.

Linear Path Queries. The first set of queries contains only expressions in which no predicate of the query tree pattern has more than one child. Such queries can be resolved using simpler data structures, e.g. path indices such as the DataGuide [15]. The performance of the hybrid system will be tested against this class of queries because it represents an important subclass of the general query class. The queries used are adopted from Kaushik et al. [19]. Query K1 is a modification of the version of the original work that returns all item entries containing the keyword "attires" rather than atomic "attires" vertices that occur below an item in order to comply with the restrictions of tree pattern expressions. Queries K2 – K4 are as described in the original research.

Point Queries. Queries Q1a and Q1b combine both structural and atomic value predicates. They essentially determine whether the given pattern exists in the data or not.

Queries with Varying Cardinality. The Queries Q2a – Q2c all locate parts of the data graph with the same structure, a profile that contains at least income, education and gender information about the person it is describing. Query Q2a represents this structural constraint alone, whereas Queries Q2b and Q2c restrict the results to subsets by means of an atomic value predicate.

Conjunctive Value Queries. Queries Q3a and Q3b both contain more than one atomic value predicate that needs to be true in combination with the structural predicates. Query Q3a looks for an item whose child nodes match three different, single valued atomic value predicates for its location, payment type and quantity. The item of Query Q3b has only one child predicate, but this predicate needs to comply with two atomic value predicates at the same time. The semantics of keyword queries represent a substring matching on the atomic value.

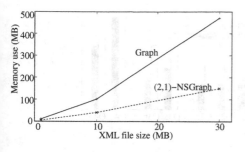

Fig. 6. Data graph and (2,1)-NSGraph

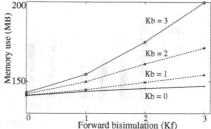

Fig. 7. Effect of varying bisimilarity

Queries Containing Regular Expressions over Nested Parts of the Source. The textual descriptions of items and categories of the XMark dataset can contain highly nested mark-up language and mixed content elements. Queries Q4a and Q4b query this part of the database for structural constraints with variable path lengths and tag label wildcards.

4 Experimental Results

4.1 Data Volumes

Merging similar nodes in the data graph restricts the overall size of the structure. The 30Mb benchmark data graph contains 1,529,075 vertices. A (2,1) bisimulation (i.e. $k_f = 2$, $k_b = 1$) of this structure reduces the size of the vertex set to 10,496 vertices. The size of the in-memory representation of the data graph and NSGraph is shown in Figures 6 and 7. Whilst the NSGraph is smaller than the data graph increased levels of bisimulation restrict this benefit.

4.2 Query Response with Fixed Bisimilarity

The first set of experiments keeps the bisimilarity structure constant, allowing a comparison of the influence of different query strategies on the data graph and NSGraph structures. The bisimulation is designed to be covering for the structural part of the most complex query not containing descendant operators, i.e. its forward bisimilarity k_f is set to the depth of the query tree pattern. Its backward bisimilarity k_b is set to one, in order to organise the atomic data by its parent's tag label. Consequently, the NSGraph used for the linear tree patterns is based on (3,1)-bisimilarity and the NSGraph used for the branching query patterns is based on (2,1)-bisimilarity.

Figure 8 summarises the performance of the set of benchmark queries on the data and NSGraphs. The number of vertices visited is an indication of the expected query cost. Although the prototype system works entirely in memory, a practical implementation working on larger datasets would need to load data from external storage. A reasonable base for performance modelling in database systems is to assume one memory read operation per vertex accessed. Consequently, the costs of loading a large but localised structure like a vertex of an

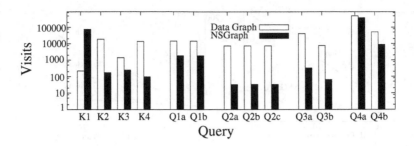

Fig. 8. Visits for each sample query on the data graph and NSGraph

NSGraph containing many entry references is usually cheaper than loading many small structures that might be spread across many different blocks. Data intensive applications operating in a wireless environment may require additional blocks of data to be fetched from the server as a consequence of an attempt to read an item not currently in storage. Restricting the number of vertices visited is therefore likely to improve the overall performance of these mobile applications.

For almost all the benchmark queries on the NSGraph fewer vertex visits are needed than for the equivalent data graph (Figure 8). The only exception to this pattern is Query K1. The performance benefit for the NSGraph is limited for this query because the atomic value predicate has a very low selectivity, returning only twenty five hits on its own, of which only five appear in the right context. Thus only a very limited fraction of the data graph is actually searched and the NSGraph cannot offer a substantial saving on this account. In addition, the NSGraph is not covering for even the structural part of this query.

4.3   Varying the Coarseness of the NSGraph Structure

The results presented in Figures 9 – 14 show the behaviour of the query classes in the context of varying bisimulation (Three-dimensional charts are necessary to show the effect that varying both the forward and backward bisimulation has on query performance). During the resolution of each query on the NSGraph, the candidate set of results has periodically to be validated, because although the graph is designed to be covering for the structural part of a query, it is not covering for tree patterns containing data predicates. The relative computational cost of the queries on the NSGraph can be estimated by the total number of entries joined in such a way because the join algorithm used has a complexity that is linear in the size of its arguments. For each query shown, both the number of vertex visits and the join cardinality patterns are presented. To aid clarity, the results for query class Q4 have been shown separately. Figures 11 and 12 present one result for each of the query classes Q1 and Q2 since there is little variation between the members of these groups. The k_b axis in Figures 9, 12 and 14 is reversed for reasons of intelligibility.

Figure 9 shows the minimal number of vertex visits taken to answer each linear query. The axes k_f and k_b determining the forward and backward bisimilarity respectively. It is clear that the number of vertices visited increases with the complexity of the bisimulation and the NSGraph based upon it. In most cases there is a significant difference between those structures based on zero backward bisimilarity and NSGraphs based on bisimilarity greater than zero. However, the increase for K1 is not monotonic. For the case where $k_f = 3$ and $k_b = 3$ there is a reduction in the number of required vertex visits. Query K1 dominates the processing costs for this set of queries because the descendant operator means that no graph based on local bisimilarity is covering even for the structural aspect of this query. For K3, the number of vertex visits grows predominantly with the backward bisimilarity length, but is independent of k_f with the exception of the case where $k_f = 0$. The minimal number of vertex visits required for Query K4 rises sharply with low values of both k_f and k_b. In contrast to the pattern of vertex visits, the total cardinality of joins required to compute the results is minimal at the point where $k_f = 3$ and $k_b = 3$ for K1 and K3 but is stable for K4.

Figures 9 and 10 suggest a trade-off exists between the precision of the NSGraph and the related I/O costs. The former is characterised by the join cardinality and the latter by the number of vertices being visited. However, there exists also a significant influence of the specific query and not only the general query class. As Figure 5 shows, the queries K1 and K4 are isomorphic as are the queries K2 and K3. Thus the observably different response to the different data groupings must be a consequence of the different selectivity of the constituent predicates.

The results obtained using the branching query classes are similar to those obtained for linear queries, which suggests that the design is equally suitable for a range of query classes. Figures 11 and 13 show the minimum number of vertices being visited for the benchmark query classes over different NSGraphs. The data confirms the results from the linear case. The number of vertices visited stabilizes for increasing backward and forward bisimilarity for Q1 and Q2 but increases monotonically for both examples of Q3. Query classes Q1 and Q2 show that even a continually growing NSGraph does not imply a continually growing number of vertices being visited.

The total number of entries being joined during query execution (Figures 12 and 14) reveals that for classes Q1 and Q2 the computational effort is minimal for maximal values of k_f and k_b. With decreasing precision in these axes, there is generally an increase in the number of candidate entries being considered although the variation caused by k_f is less consistent for low values of k_b. In the remaining query classes, the join cardinality is usually most favourable at high k_b and relatively independent of k_f.

The response of classes Q3 and Q4 show that for both the vertex visits and the join cardinality, members of the same query class can return different response patterns over the bisimulation range presented.

5 Discussion and Conclusion

The results in Figure 8 show that when the bisimulation is held constant the number of reads is generally less for the NSGraph than for the data graph.

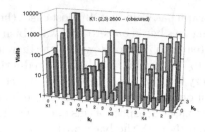 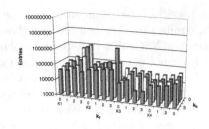

Fig. 9. Vertices visited for linear queries   **Fig. 10.** Join cardinality for linear queries

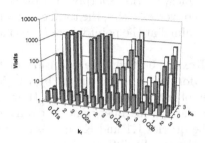 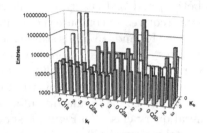

Fig. 11. Vertices visited for branch queries **Fig. 12.** Join cardinality for branch queries

This is a consequence of the localisation of data within the NSGraph, where queries are themselves very limited in the data that they need to access (such as K1) the NSGraph does not perform as well as the data graph. In terms of the computational effort needed to resolve queries over these structures, the data graph has an advantage. These experiments were carried out on memory resident data structures. Larger disk-based structures would make performance more dependent on I/O and therefore show more of an advantage of the NSGraph in both types of query.

The effect of increasing levels of bisimulation both in a forward and backward direction is to group together elements with increasingly similar structures. Partitioning dictionaries using the same approach similarly results in an increasing number of separate dictionary structures. Figures 9, 11 and 13 show that the number of visits needed to resolve the sample queries generally increases in association with increasing levels of bisimulation. The implication of the general trend is therefore that in a mobile pull-based system, the number of cache faults will usually be minimised by limiting the level of bisimulation. This is consistent with the outcome that could be expected from increasing the fragmentation of the data structure representation.

Different query classes show variations in response to different levels of bisimulation. Increasing either the forward or backward bisimulation, whilst keeping the remaining dimension at zero, does not significantly increase the number of visits for some queries (e.g. Q1a). Queries such as K3 and the classes Q1 and Q2 do not benefit significantly from very precise NSGraphs (cases with $k_f > 1$ and $k_b > 1$). Other queries (such as K1) do not show this pattern and the vertex visits needed increase markedly from low levels of bisimulation. Particularly

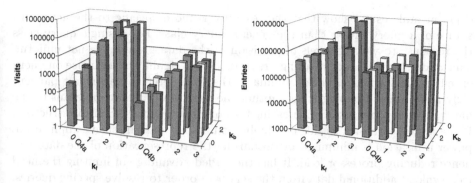

Fig. 13. Vertices visited for nested queries

Fig. 14. Join cardinality for nested queries

useful points exist in this space such as $k_f = 3$ and $k_b = 3$, which minimise both the likely cache faults and the computational load.

The most common pattern shown in Figures 8–14 suggest that query processing on the NSGraph trades graph precision with the number of vertices being visited. There are, however data sets where the cardinality and hence computational cost remain constant while the number of vertices that need to be visited increases. Figures 9 and 10 show that linear query K1, cannot make use of the advantages of the NSGraph, i.e. it solely relies on the tag label and data indices provided.

The implementation of the experimental system covers a subset of the total functionality possible. Tree pattern queries can be answered using the current system but it does not generalise to unrestricted branching path expressions. The in-memory implementation of the data structure limits the maximal size of the data being queried and also affects the relative influence of processing and I/O costs on the total query time. For the experimental system, the costs of string matching and merge-joins dominate the overall costs, whereas for a disk-based system the I/O performance would play a bigger role. The system retains the same structure as the basic XML document (although in abbreviated form) and can consequently be updated using similar techniques. Insertion into or update of dictionaries may occasionally require restructuring and we plan to investigate how best to minimise the effects of this.

The results described here were derived using a bottom up approach to embedding the query into the NSGraph structure. It would be possible to use a top down variant of such an approach as well as a merge join algorithm. These algorithms are likely to produce performance results that differ from those presented here and may provide opportunities for further improvements.

The hybrid query system is able to deal with queries containing both structural and atomic value predicates without the need to preserve the original XML data structure. It shows how to combine two different data groupings, each of which was previously shown to provide an efficient solution for separate problems. A numbering scheme for the nodes of the distinct spanning tree combines the two partial solutions and allows for an easy transition between them. The experimental results show that the response is more specific to the actual instance of a query rather than the general query class. For a single query class the response to varying levels of precision of the data grouping is not uniform. The cardinality of its constituting predicates has a significant influence on query execution performance. Local minima in the parameter space suggest particularly useful data groupings that capture the aspects of a source relevant to the query without unnecessarily increasing the complexity of the NSGraph structure. Using a structure such as this in a mobile pull-based data intensive application, power utilisation is minimised by optimising the representation of the data and hence reducing processor load. It has the added advantage of limiting the need to download additional data from the server in order to resolve specific queries.

References

1. G. Amato, F. Debole, P. Zezula, and F. Rabitti. YAPI: Yet another path index for xml searching. In *Proc of ECDL*, pages 176 – 187, 2003.
2. A. Arion, A. Bonifati, G. Costa, S. D'Aguanno, I. Manolescu, and A. Pugliese. Xquec: Pushing queries to compressed xml data. In *VLDB*, pages 1065–1068, 2003.
3. N. Bruno, N. Koudas, and D. Srivastava. Holistic twig joins: Optimal XML pattern matching. In *Proc. of SIGMOD*, pages 310–321, 2002.
4. P. Buneman, M. Grohe, and C. Koch. Path queries on compressed XML. In *Proc. of VLDB*, pages 141–152, 2003.
5. P. Buneman, B. Choi, W. Fan, R. Hutchison, R. Mann, and S. D. Viglas. Vectorizing and querying large xml repositories. In *ICDE'05: Proceedings of the 21st International Conference on Data Engineering*, pages 261–272, 2005. IEEE Computer Society.
6. P. Buneman, S. B. Davidson, M. F. Fernandez, and D. Suciu. Adding structure to unstructured data. In *ICDT '97: Proceedings of the 6th International Conference on Database Theory*, pages 336–350, 1997. Springer-Verlag.
7. Q. Chen, A. Lim, and K. W. Ong. D(k)-index: an adaptive structural summary for graph-structured data. In *SIGMOD '03: Proceedings of the 2003 ACM SIGMOD international conference on Management of data*, pages 134–144, 2003. ACM Press.
8. J. Cheney. Compressing xml with multiplexed hierarchical ppm models. In *Data Compression Conference*, pages 163–, 2001.
9. J. Cheney. Tradeoffs in xml database compression. In *DCC*, pages 392–401, 2006.
10. J. Cheng and W. Ng. Xqzip: Querying compressed xml using structural indexing. In *EDBT*, pages 219–236, 2004.
11. S. Y. Chien, Z. Vagena, et al. Efficient structural joins on indexed XML documents. In *Proc. of VLDB*, pages 263–274, 2002.
12. B. Choi and P. Buneman. XML vectorization: A column-based XML storage model. Technical Report MS-CIS-03-17, University of Pennsylvania, 2003.
13. P. F. Dietz. Maintaining order in a linked list. In *Proc. of STOCS*, pages 122–127, 1982.
14. P. Ferragina, F. Luccio, G. Manzini, and S. Muthukrishnan. Compressing and searching xml data via two zips. In *Proc. World Wide Web Conference 2006 (WWW'06)*, 2006.
15. R. Goldman and J. Widom. DataGuides: Enabling query formulation and optimization in semistructured databases. In *Proc. of VLDB*, pages 436–445, 1997.

16. T. Grust. Accelerating XPath location steps. In *Proc. of SIGMOD*, pages 109–120, 2002.

17. A. Halverson, J. Burger, et al. Mixed mode XML query processing. In *Proc of VLDB*, pages 225–236, 2003.

18. R. Kaushik, P Bohannon, et al. Covering indexes for branching path queries. In *Proc. of SIGMOD*, pages 133–144, 2002.

19. R. Kaushik, R. Krishnamurthy, et al. On the integration of structure indexes and inverted lists. In *Proc. of SIGMOD*, pages 779–790, 2004.

20. R. Kaushik, P. Shenoy, et al. Exploiting local similarity for indexing paths in graph-structured data. In *Proc. of ICDE*, pages 129–140, 2002.

21. D. D. Kha, M. Yoshikawa, and S. Uemura. A structural numbering scheme for XML data. In *Proc. of EDBT*, pages 279–289, 2001.

22. J. Lee, Y. Lee, S. Kang, H. Jin, S. Lee, B. Kim, and J. Song. Bmq-index: Shared and incremental processing of border monitoring queries over data streams. In *The 7th International Conference on Mobile Data Management (MDM'06)*, 2006.

23. Q. Li and B. Moon. Indexing and querying XML data for regular path expressions. In *Proc. of VLDB*, pages 361–370, 2001.

24. H. Liefke and D. Suciu. XMill: An efficient compressor for XML data. In *Proc. of SIGMOD*, pages 153–164, 2000.

25. J. McHugh and J. Widom. Query optimization for XML. In *Proc. of VLDB*, pages 315–326, 1999.

26. J-K. Min, M-J. Park, and C-W. Chung. Xpress: A queriable compression for xml data. In *SIGMOD Conference*, pages 122–133, 2003.

27. J F. Naughton, D. J. DeWitt, et al. The Niagara internet query system. *IEEE Data Eng. Bull.*, 24(2):27–33, 2001.

28. M. Neumüller and J N. Wilson. Improving XML processing using adapted data structures. In *Proc. of WEBDB*, pages 63–77, 2002.

29. A. R. Schmidt, F. Waas, et al. XMark: A benchmark for XML data management. In *Proc. of VLDB*, pages 27–32, 2002.

30. P. M. Tolani and J. R. Haritsa. Xgrind: A query-friendly xml compressor. In *ICDE*, pages 225–234, 2002.

31. W. Wang, H. Jiang, H. Wang, X. Lin, H. Lu and J. Li. Efficient processing of XML path queries using the disk-based F&B Index. In *Proc. of VLDB*, pages 145–156, 2005.

32. X. Yan, P. S. Yu, and J. Han. Graph indexing: a frequent structure-based approach. In *SIGMOD '04: Proceedings of the 2004 ACM SIGMOD international conference on Management of data*, pages 335–346, New York, NY, USA, 2004. ACM Press.

33. P. Zezula, G. Amato, et al. Tree signatures for XML querying and navigation. In *Proc. of XSym*, pages 149–163, 2003.

34. C. Zhang, J F. Naughton, et al. On supporting containment queries in relational database management systems. In *Proc. of SIGMOD*, pages 425–436, 2001.

35. N. Zhang, M. T. Ozsu, I. F. Ilyas, A. Aboulnaga, and D. R. Cheriton. Fix: Feature-based indexing technique for xml documents. Technical Report CS-2006-07, School of Computer Science, University of Waterloo, 2006.

On the Expressive Power of XQuery-Based Update Languages

Jan Hidders, Jan Paredaens, and Roel Vercammen*

University of Antwerp

Abstract. XQuery 1.0, the XML query language which is about to become a W3C Recommendation, lacks the ability to make persistent changes to instances of its data model. A number of proposals to extend XQuery with update facilities have been made lately, including a W3C Working Draft. In order to investigate some of the different constructs that are introduced in these proposals, we define an XQuery-based update language that combines them. By doing so, we show that it is possible to give a concise, complete and formal definition of such a language. We define subsets of this language to examine the relative expressive power of the different constructs, and we establish the relationships between these subsets in terms of queries and updates that can be expressed. Finally, we discuss the relationships between these subsets and existing XQuery-based update languages.

1   Introduction

With the growing acceptance of XQuery as the main query language for XML data, there has also been a growing need for an extension that allows updates. This has lead to several proposals such as [11], [9], UpdateX [10,1], XQuery! [3] and the XQuery Update Facility [2]. Next to introducing operations for manipulating nodes such as inserting and deleting, these proposals often also introduce special operations such as the snap operation (in XQuery!) and the transform operation (in XQuery Update Facility) to extend the expressive power of the language, sometimes for queries as well as updates. For example, the snap operation allows us write queries in XQuery that use side effects and bounded iteration. Another example is the transform operation that allows us to concisely express a transformation that copies an entire tree and makes a few minor changes to it. In this paper we investigate the relative expressive power of such constructs for expressing queries as well as updates. In addition we examine the strict separation of expressions in updating and non-updating expressions, and determine whether this influences the ability to express certain queries and updates.

To investigate the mentioned questions we define LiXQuery$^+$ by taking LiXQuery[7], a concise and formally defined subset of XQuery, and extending it with all the mentioned constructs.

---

* Roel Vercammen is supported by IWT – Institute for the Encouragement of Innovation by Science and Technology Flanders, grant number 33581.

S. Amer-Yahia et al. (Eds.): XSym 2006, LNCS 4156, pp. 92–106, 2006.

The remainder of this paper is organized as follows. Section 2 presents the syntax of LiXQuery[+] and discusses its semantics informally. Section 3 presents the formal framework necessary for defining the semantics. Section 4 defines the semantics of expressions in LiXQuery[+]. Section 5 presents the results on the expressive power of the different constructs [1] . Section 6 relates these results to existing proposals in the literature and finally Section 7 contains the conclusion.

2   Syntax and Informal Semantics

Due to space limitations, we do not give the complete LiXQuery[+] syntax, but only show how to extend the LiXQuery grammar to obtain LiXQuery[+]. We start from the grammar as given in [4], remove the start symbol ⟨Query⟩ and introduce a new start symbol ⟨Program⟩, which is a sequence of variable and function declarations followed by an expression. The syntax of LiXQuery[+] programs is given in Fig. 1 as an abstract syntax, i.e., it assumes that extra brackets and precedence rules are added for disambiguation. The ellipsis in the non-terminal ⟨Expr⟩ refer to the right-hand side of this non-terminal in the LiXQuery grammar. The XQuery features that we can express in non-recursive LiXQuery include FLWOR-expressions, path expressions, typeswitches, node and value comparisons, sequence generations (using the "to"-operation), sequence concatenation, and some simple arithmetic.

⟨Program⟩	::=	(((⟨VarDecl⟩ | ⟨FunDecl⟩) ";")* ⟨Expr⟩
⟨VarDecl⟩	::=	"declare" "variable" ⟨Var⟩ ":=" ⟨Expr⟩
⟨FunDecl⟩	::=	"declare" "function" ⟨Name⟩ "(" ((⟨Var⟩ ("," ⟨Var⟩)*)? ")" "{" ⟨Expr⟩ "}"
⟨Expr⟩	::=	... | ⟨Insert⟩ | ⟨Rename⟩ | ⟨Replace⟩ | ⟨Delete⟩ | ⟨Snap⟩ | ⟨Transform⟩
⟨Insert⟩	::=	"insert" ⟨Expr⟩ ("into" | "before" | "after") ⟨Expr⟩
⟨Rename⟩	::=	"rename" ⟨Expr⟩ "as" ⟨Expr⟩
⟨Replace⟩	::=	"replace" "value" "of" ⟨Expr⟩ "with" ⟨Expr⟩
⟨Delete⟩	::=	"delete" ⟨Expr⟩
⟨Snap⟩	::=	"snap" (("unordered" ("nondeterministic" | "deterministic")) | "ordered") "{" ⟨Expr⟩ "}"
⟨Transform⟩	::=	"transform" "copy" ⟨Var⟩ ":=" ⟨Expr⟩ "modify" ⟨Expr⟩ "return" ⟨Expr⟩

Fig. 1. Syntax of LiXQuery[+]

We assume the reader is already familiar with XQuery. We therefore only describe the semantics of the new expressions and sketch the modifications to the semantics of the other expressions.

We first describe the semantics of the update expressions, i.e., the "insert", "rename", "replace" and "delete" operations. The "insert" operation makes a copy of the nodes in the result of the first expression and adds these (afterwards) at the position that is indicated by either "into", "before", or "after" and which is relative to the singleton result node of the second expression. The "rename" operation renames an element or an attribute, and the "replace" operation replaces the value of a text or an attribute node with a new atomic

---

[1] We only give sketches of the proofs, for the full proofs we refer to [5].

value. Both operations are node-identity preserving, i.e., the identity of the updates node is not changed. The "delete" expression removes the incoming edges for a set of nodes, which can then be garbage collected iff they are not accessible anymore through variable bindings or the result sequence.

For most expressions we assume a snapshot semantics, which intuitively means that a snapshot of the store is being made before the evaluation of the expression and the resulting updates are not yet performed, but instead they are added to a list of pending updates. There are four exceptions to this: the "snap" operation, expressions at the end of a program, expressions at the right-hand side of a variable declaration and the "transform" expression. We discuss these four cases in the following.

A "snap" operation applies the list of pending updates that is generated by the subexpression to the store and returns an empty update list. If the snap expression contains the keyword "ordered", then the pending updates are applied in the same order as they were generated. Else the order of application is undefined and the keywords "deterministic" and "nondeterministic" specify whether the order of the application of pending updates is allowed to affect the set of possible result stores. As an illustration of the "snap" expression consider:

```
for $d in //dept return (
  snap ordered { replace value of $d/salarytotal with 0 },
  for $e in $d/emp return
    snap ordered {
      replace value of $d/salarytotal
      with $d/salarytotal + $e/salarytotal } )
```

This expression computes for each department the total of the salaries of its employees. Note that if we replace the two "snap" operations with one big "snap" operation around the whole expression then it will compute for each department the salary of the last employee since the value of $d/salarytotal is not updated during the evaluation.

When evaluating an expression at the end of a program or the right-hand side of a variable declaration, an implicit top-level "snap ordered" is presumed, i.e., the list of pending updates that is generated by the expression is applied to the store.

The final exception to the snapshot semantics is the "transform" operation. It makes a deep copy of the result of the first subexpression, evaluates the second subexpression and applies the resulting pending updates provided these are only on the deep copy, and finally evaluates the return clause and returns its result. As an illustration of the "transform" expression consider:

```
transform copy $d := //dept[@name = "Security"]
          modify delete $d//*[@security-level > 3]
          return $d
```

This expression retrieves all information about the security department except the subtrees which have a security level higher than three. Note that the transform operation cannot update an existing fragment in the XML store.

Finally, all other operations were already in LiXQuery and their semantics is now extended in such a way that the result is not only the result sequence, but also the concatenation of all lists of pending updates that were generated during the evaluations of subexpressions.

3   Formal Framework

We now proceed with the formal semantics of LiXQuery$^+$. Due to space limitations, we will not fully introduce all concepts of LiXQuery here, but refer to [7] for some examples and a more elaborated introduction. We assume a set of *strings* S and a set of *names* $N \subseteq S$, which contains those strings that may be used as tag names. The set of all atomic values is denotes by A and is a superset of S. We also assume four countably infinite sets of nodes V^d, V^e, V^a and V^t which respectively represent the set of *document, element, attribute* and *text nodes*. These sets are pairwise disjoint with each other and the set of atomic values. The set of all nodes is denoted as V, i.e., $V = V^d \cup V^e \cup V^a \cup V^t$. In the rest of this paper, we use the following notation: v for values, x for items, n for nodes, r for roots, s for strings and names, f for function names, b for booleans , i for integers, e for expressions and p for programs. We denote the empty sequence as $\langle \rangle$, non-empty sequences as for example $\langle 1, 2, 3 \rangle$ and the concatenation of two sequences l_1 and l_2 as $l_1 \circ l_2$. Finally, if l is a list or sequence, then the set of items in l is denoted as $\mathbf{Set}(l)$ and the bag (unordered list) representation of l is denoted by $\mathbf{Bag}(l)$.

3.1   XML Store

Expressions are evaluated against an *XML store* which contains XML fragments. This store contains the fragments that are created as intermediate results, but also the web documents that are accessed by the expression. Although in practice these documents are materialized in the store when they are accessed for the first time, we assume here that all documents are in fact already in the store when the expression is evaluated.

Definition 1 (XML Store). *An XML store is a 6-tuple $St = (V, E, \ll, \nu, \sigma, \delta)$:*

- V *is a finite subset of V^2;*
- (V, E) *is a directed acyclic graph where each node has an in-degree of at most one, and hence it is composed of trees; if $(m, n) \in E$ then we say that n is a child of m; we denote by E^* the reflexive transitive closure of E;*
- $\ll$ *is a total order on the nodes of V;*
- $\nu : V^e \cup V^a \to N$ *labels element and attribute nodes with their node name;*
- $\sigma : V^a \cup V^t \to S$ *labels attribute and text nodes with their string value;*
- $\delta : S \to V^d$ *a partial function that associates a URI with a document node.*

Moreover, some additional properties must hold for such a tuple in order to be a valid XML store. We refer to the technical report [6] on LiXQuery$^+$ for these properties.

Note that this definition slightly differs from our original definition of an XML Store [7], since we now have included the document order in the store instead of the sibling order. In the rest of this paper we will write V_{St} to denote the set of nodes of the store St, and similarly we write E_{St}, $\ll_{St}$, ν_{St}, σ_{St} and δ_{St} to denote respectively the second to the sixth component of the 6-tuple St.

---

[2] We write V^d to denote $V \cap V^d$, and use a similar notation for V^e, V^a, and V^t.

3.2   Evaluation Environment

Expressions are evaluated against an environment. Assuming that $\mathcal{X}$ is the set of LiXQuery$^+$-expressions this environment is defined as follows.

Definition 2 (Environment). *An environment of an XML store St is a tuple $En = (\mathbf{a}, \mathbf{b}, \mathbf{v}, \mathbf{x})$ with a partial function $\mathbf{a} : \mathcal{N} \to \mathcal{N}^*$ that maps a function name to its formal arguments, a partial function $\mathbf{b} : \mathcal{N} \to \mathcal{X}$ that maps a function name to the body of the function, a partial function $\mathbf{v} : \mathcal{N} \to (\mathcal{V} \cup \mathcal{A})^*$ that maps variable names to their values, and $\mathbf{x}$ which is either undefined ($\bot$) or an item of St and indicates the context item.*

If En is an environment, n a name and y an item then we let $En[\mathbf{a}(n) \mapsto y]$ ($En[\mathbf{b}(n) \mapsto y]$, $En[\mathbf{v}(n) \mapsto y]$) denote the environment that is equal to En except that the function $\mathbf{a}$ ($\mathbf{b}$, $\mathbf{v}$) maps n to y. Similarly, we let $En[\mathbf{x} \mapsto y]$ denote the environment that is equal to En except that $\mathbf{x}$ is defined as y if $y \neq \bot$ and undefined otherwise.

3.3   List of Pending Updates

A new concept in the LiXQuery$^+$ semantics, when compared to LiXQuery, is the list of pending updates. This list contains a number of primitive update operations which have to be performed after the evaluation of the entire expression.

Definition 3 (Primitive Update Operations). *Let $n, n_1, \ldots, n_m$ be nodes in a store St, and $s \in \mathcal{S}$. A primitive update operation on the store St is one of following operations: $insBef(n, \langle n_1, \ldots, n_m \rangle)$, $insAft(n, \langle n_1, \ldots, n_m \rangle)$, $insInto(n, \langle n_1, \ldots, n_m \rangle)$, $ren(n, s)$, $repVal(n, s)$, $del(n)$.*

Before proceeding with the formal semantics, we first give some intuition about these primitive update operations. The operation $insBef$ ($insAft$, $insInto$) moves nodes n_1 to n_m before (after, into) the node n. In the formal semantics of LiXQuery$^+$, we will see that the nodes n_1 to n_m are always copies of other nodes. Note that the operation $insInto$ can have several result stores, since the list of nodes can be inserted in an arbitrary position among the children. The operations ren and $repVal$ change respectively the name and the value of n to s. Finally, the operation del removes the incoming edge from n and hence detaches the subtree rooted at n. Note that del can, similar to $insInto$, have more than one result store, due to the resulting document order. More precisely, the subtree that is detached by a del operation has to be given another place in document order, since otherwise this tree would be mixed in document order with the tree from which we deleted the edge, which is a violation of one of the additional properties of Definition 1. The exact location in document order of the detached subtree is chosen in a non-deterministic manner.

We write $St \vdash o \Rightarrow^{\mathsf{U}} St'$ to denote that applying the primitive update operation o to St can result in the store St'. The definition of $\Rightarrow^{\mathsf{U}}$ is given in Fig. 2 by means of inference rules. Each rule consists of a set of premises and a conclusion

$$\frac{St' = St[\nu(n) \mapsto s]}{St \vdash ren(n,s) \Rightarrow^U St'}$$

$$\frac{St' = St[\sigma(n) \mapsto s]}{St \vdash repVal(n,s) \Rightarrow^U St''}$$

$$\frac{St' = (St \setminus n) \cup St[n]}{St \vdash del(n) \Rightarrow^U St'}$$

$$\frac{\begin{array}{cccc} St \setminus n_1 \setminus \ldots \setminus n_m = St' \setminus n_1 \setminus \ldots \setminus n_m = St'' \\ St[n_1]=St'[n_1] & \ldots & St[n_m]=St'[n_m] \\ (n,n_1)\in E_{St'} & \ldots & (n,n_m)\in E_{St'} \\ n_1 \ll_{St'} n_2 & \ldots & n_{m-1}\ll_{St'} n_m \end{array}}{St \vdash insInto(n,\langle n_1,\ldots,n_m\rangle)\Rightarrow^U St'}$$

$$\frac{\begin{array}{cccc} n_1,\ldots,n_m \in \mathcal{V}^e \cup \mathcal{V}^t \\ St\setminus n_1\setminus\ldots\setminus n_m = St'\setminus n_1\setminus\ldots\setminus n_m = St'' \\ St[n_1]=St'[n_1] & \ldots & St[n_m]=St'[n_m] \\ n'\in V_{St''}\Rightarrow(n\ll_{St'} n' \Leftrightarrow n_m \ll_{St'} n') \\ n\ll_{St'} n_1 \\ n_1\ll_{St'} n_2 & \ldots & n_{m-1}\ll_{St'} n_m \end{array}}{St\vdash insAft(n,\langle n_1,\ldots,n_m\rangle)\Rightarrow^U St'}$$

$$\frac{\begin{array}{cccc} n_1,\ldots,n_m\in\mathcal{V}^e\cup\mathcal{V}^t \\ St\setminus n_1\setminus\ldots\setminus n_m=St'\setminus n_1\setminus\ldots\setminus n_m=St'' \\ St[n_1]=St'[n_1] & \ldots & St[n_m]=St'[n_m] \\ n'\in V_{St''}\Rightarrow(n'\ll_{St'} n\Leftrightarrow n'\ll_{St'} n_1) \\ n_m\ll_{St'} n \\ n_1\ll_{St'} n_2 & \ldots & n_{m-1}\ll_{St'} n_m \end{array}}{St\vdash insBef(n,\langle n_1,\ldots,n_m\rangle)\Rightarrow^U St'}$$

Fig. 2. Semantics of the Primitive Update Operations

of the form $St \vdash o \Rightarrow^U St'$. The free variables in the rules are always assumed to be universally quantified. In these rules we use some additional notations, which we will now explain.

Let St be a store and n an element of V_{St}. We define V_{St}^n as $\{n'|(n,n')\in E_{St}^*\}$, i.e., the set of nodes in the subtree rooted at n in St. The projection of St to a set of nodes N is denoted by $\Pi_N(St)$ and is the restriction of all components of St to N instead of V_{St}. The restriction of St to n is defined as $\Pi_{V_{St}^n}(St)$ and is denoted by $St[n]$. The exclusion of n from St is defined as $\Pi_{V_{St}-V_{St}^n}(St)$ and is denoted by $St \setminus n$. For both restriction and exclusion it is not hard to see that the projection always results in a store. Finally, if St is a store, n a node in St, and s a string, then we let $St[\delta(n) \mapsto s]$ $(St[\nu(n) \mapsto s])$ denote the store that is equal to St except that $\delta_{St'}(n) = s$ $(\nu_{St'}(n) = s)$.

We now define *a list l of pending updates over a store St* as a list of primitive update operations on St. The set of affected nodes of l is denoted by **Targets**(l) and defined as the set of nodes that occur as the first argument in a primitive update operation appearing in l.

The notation $St \vdash o \Rightarrow^U St'$, used to specify the semantics of primitive update operations, is overloaded for sequences of primitive update operations. For such a sequence $l = \langle o_1,\ldots,o_m\rangle$ we define $St \vdash l \Rightarrow^U St'$ by induction on m such that (1) $St \vdash \langle\rangle \Rightarrow^U St$ and (2) if $St \vdash \langle o_1,\ldots,o_{m-1}\rangle \Rightarrow^U St'$ and $St' \vdash o_m \Rightarrow^U St''$ then $St \vdash \langle o_1,\ldots,o_m\rangle \Rightarrow^U St''$.

For some lists of pending updates, we can reorder the application of these primitive update operations without changing the semantics. Therefore we say that l is *execution-order independent* if for every sequences l' such that **Bag**$(l) =$ **Bag**(l') and store St' it holds that $St \vdash l \Rightarrow^U St'$ iff $St \vdash l' \Rightarrow^U St'$.

Finally, the following lemma gives an algorithm to decide execution-order independence of a list of pending updates:

Lemma 1. *A list of pending updates $l = \langle o_1,\ldots,o_m\rangle$ over a store St is execution-order dependent iff there are two primitive update operations o_i and o_j in l such that*

$i \neq j$, and there are $n, n_1, \ldots, n_m, n'_1, \ldots, n'_l \in V_{St}$ and $s, s' \in S$, such that $s \neq s'$, $\langle n_1, \ldots, n_m \rangle \neq \langle n'_1, \ldots, n'_l \rangle$ and one of the following holds:
- $o_i = ren(n, s) \wedge o_j = ren(n, s')$
- $o_i = repVal(n, s) \wedge o_j = repVal(n, s')$
- $o_i = insBef(n, \langle n_1, \ldots, n_m \rangle) \wedge o_j = insBef(n, \langle n'_1, \ldots, n'_l \rangle)$
- $o_i = insAft(n, \langle n_1, \ldots, n_m \rangle) \wedge o_j = insAft(n, \langle n'_1, \ldots, n'_l \rangle)$

3.4 Program Semantics

We now define the semantics of programs. We write $(St, En) \vdash p \Rightarrow (St', v)$ to denote that the *program p*, evaluated against the XML store St and environment En of St, can result in the new XML store St' and value v of St'. Similarly, $(St, En) \vdash e \Rightarrow^E (St', v, l)$ means that the evaluation of *expression e* against St and En may result in St', v, and the list of pending updates l over St'. The semantics of expressions is given in Section 4. Finally, the semantics of a program is defined by following reasoning rules:

$$\frac{St, En[\mathbf{a}(f) \mapsto \langle s_1, \ldots s_m \rangle][\mathbf{b}(f) \mapsto e] \vdash p \Rightarrow (St', v')}{St, En \vdash \texttt{declare function } f \ (\$s_1, \ldots, \$s_m)\{ \ e \ \} \ ; \ p \Rightarrow (St', v')}$$

$$\frac{St, En \vdash e \Rightarrow (St', v) \qquad St', En[\mathbf{v}(s) \mapsto v] \vdash p \Rightarrow (St'', v'')}{St, En \vdash \texttt{declare variable } \$s := e \ ; \ p \Rightarrow (St'', v'')}$$

$$\frac{(St, En) \vdash e \Rightarrow^E (St', v, l) \qquad St' \vdash l \Rightarrow^U St''}{(St, En) \vdash e \Rightarrow (St'', v)}$$

Note that in the last rule, v is a value of St'', since $V_{St'} = V_{St''}$.

3.5 Auxiliary Notions

We conclude this section by giving some notational tools for the rest of this paper. First, we define some auxiliary operations on stores.

Two stores St and St' are disjoint, denoted as $St \cap St' = \emptyset$, iff $V_{St} \cap V_{St'} = \emptyset$. The definition of the *union* of two disjoint stores St and St', denoted as $St \cup St'$, is straightforward. The resulting document order is extended to a total order in a nondeterministic way.

An *item* of an XML store St is an atomic value in $\mathcal{A}$ or a node in St. Given a sequence of nodes l in an XML store St we let $\mathbf{Ord}_{St}(l)$ denote the unique sequence $l' = \langle y_1, \ldots, y_m \rangle$ such that $\mathbf{Set}(l) = \mathbf{Set}(l')$ and $y_1 \ll_{St} \cdots \ll_{St} y_m$.

Two trees defined by two nodes n_1 and n_2 in a store St can be equal up to node identity, in which case we say that they are *deep equal* and denote this as $\mathbf{DpEq}_{St}(n_1, n_2)$.

4 Semantics of Expressions

Similar to LiXQuery, the semantics of LiXQuery$^+$ expressions is specified by means of inference rules. Each rule consists of a set of premises and a conclusion of the form $(St, En) \vdash e \Rightarrow^E (St', v, l)$. The free variables in the rules are assumed to be universally quantified. Due to the lack of space we only give the rules for the expressions that are new in LiXQuery$^+$ and illustrate how the other rules can be obtained.

4.1 Basic Update Expressions

The `delete` results into a set of pending updates which will delete the incoming edges of the selected nodes.

$$\frac{(St, En) \vdash e \Rightarrow^{E} (St_1, \langle n_1, \ldots, n_m \rangle, l)}{(St, En) \vdash \mathtt{delete}\ e \Rightarrow^{E} (St_1, \langle\rangle, l \circ \langle del(n_1), \ldots, del(n_m) \rangle)}$$

The `rename` and `replace value` expressions evaluate two subexpressions which have to result in respectively one node and one string value. Similar to the `delete` expression we add new primitive operation to the list of pending updates. For the exact inference rules we refer to the technical report[6]. An `insert` expression makes a copy of the nodes that are selected by the first subexpression and puts these copies at a certain place w.r.t. the node that is returned by the second expression. The position is indicated by either "before", "after", or "into". In case of insertion into a node n, the relative place of the copied nodes among the children of n is chosen arbitrarily, but the relative order of the copies has to be preserved. We show the semantics for the "insert ... into ..." expression.

$$\frac{\begin{array}{c} (St, En) \vdash e_1 \Rightarrow^{E} (St_1, \langle n \rangle, l_1) \\ (St_1, En) \vdash e_2 \Rightarrow^{E} (St_2, \langle n_1, \ldots, n_m \rangle, l_2) \quad St' = St_2 \cup St'_1 \cup \ldots \cup St'_m \\ \mathbf{DpEq}_{St'}(n_1, n'_1) \ \ldots \ \mathbf{DpEq}_{St'}(n_m, n'_m) \quad V^{n'_1}_{St'_1} = V_{St'_1} \ \ldots \ V^{n'_m}_{St'_m} = V_{St'_m} \end{array}}{(St, En) \vdash \mathtt{insert}\ e_2\ \mathtt{into}\ e_1 \Rightarrow^{E} (St_3, \langle\rangle, l_1 \circ l_2 \circ \langle insInto(n, \langle n'_1, \ldots, n'_m \rangle) \rangle)}$$

4.2 Snap Expression

The snap operation comes in three different flavours: ordered, unordered deterministic and unordered nondeterministic. The ordered mode specifies that the pending updates have to be applied in the same order as they were generated, the unordered deterministic mode requires that the list of pending updates has to be execution-order independent, while the unordered nondeterministic mode applies the pending updates in an arbitrary order.

$$\frac{(St, En) \vdash e \Rightarrow^{E} (St', v, l) \quad St' \vdash l \Rightarrow^{U} St''}{(St, En) \vdash \mathtt{snap\ ordered}\ \{\ e\ \} \Rightarrow^{E} (St'', v, \langle\rangle)}$$

$$\frac{(St, En) \vdash e \Rightarrow^{E} (St', v, l) \quad \mathbf{Bag}(l) = \mathbf{Bag}(l') \quad St' \vdash l' \Rightarrow^{U} St''}{(St, En) \vdash \mathtt{snap\ unordered\ nondeterministic}\ \{\ e\ \} \Rightarrow^{E} (St'', v, \langle\rangle)}$$

$$\frac{\begin{array}{c} (St, En) \vdash e \Rightarrow^{E} (St', v, l) \\ l\ is\ execution\text{-}order\ independent \quad \mathbf{Bag}(l) = \mathbf{Bag}(l') \quad St' \vdash l' \Rightarrow^{U} St'' \end{array}}{(St, En) \vdash \mathtt{snap\ unordered\ deterministic}\ \{\ e\ \} \Rightarrow^{E} (St'', v, \langle\rangle)}$$

4.3 Transform Expression

The transform expression first evaluates the first subexpression which should result in a sequence of nodes. Then it makes deep copies of each of these nodes, placed relatively in document order as the original nodes were ordered in the result sequence. The second subexpression is evaluated with the variable bound to the deep-copied nodes, and if the resulting list of pending updates only affects nodes in the deep copies then these are applied to the store and the last subexpression is evaluated.

$$
\frac{
\begin{array}{c}
(St, En) \vdash e_1 \Rightarrow^E (St_1, \langle n_1, \ldots, n_m \rangle, \langle \rangle) \\
St'_1 = St_1 \cup St_{1,1} \cup \ldots \cup St_{1,m} \quad \mathbf{DpEq}_{St'_1}(n_1, n'_1) \ \ldots \ \mathbf{DpEq}_{St'_1}(n_m, n'_m) \\
V^{n'_1}_{St_{1,1}} = V_{St_{1,1}} \ \ldots \ V^{n'_m}_{St_{1,m}} = V_{St_{1,m}} \quad n'_1 \ll_{St'_1} n'_2 \ll_{St'_1} \ldots \ll_{St'_1} n'_m \\
En_1 = En[\mathbf{v}(s) \mapsto \langle n'_1, \ldots, n'_m \rangle)] \quad (St'_1, En_1) \vdash e_2 \Rightarrow^E (St_2, v, l) \\
\mathbf{Targets}(l) \subseteq V_{St'_1} - V_{St_1} \quad St_2 \vdash l \Rightarrow^U St'_2 \quad (St'_2, En_1) \vdash e_3 \Rightarrow^E (St_3, v', \langle \rangle)
\end{array}
}{
(St, En) \vdash \mathtt{transform\ copy\ } \$s := e_1 \mathtt{\ modify\ } e_2 \mathtt{\ return\ } e_3 \Rightarrow^E (St_3, v', \langle \rangle)
}
$$

4.4 Other Expressions

To illustrate the semantics of expressions already in LiXQuery we present the reasoning rules for the concatenation and the for-expression. The other rules can be obtained from those in [7] in a similar way by extending them such that the lists of pending updates of the subexpressions are concatenated.

$$
\frac{(St, En) \vdash e_1 \Rightarrow^E (St_1, v_1, l_1) \quad (St_1, En) \vdash e_2 \Rightarrow^E (St_2, v_2, l_2)}{(St, En) \vdash e_1, e_2 \Rightarrow^E (St_2, v_1 \circ v_2, l_1 \circ l_2)}
$$

$$
\frac{
\begin{array}{c}
(St, En) \vdash e \Rightarrow^E (St_0, \langle x_1, \ldots, x_m \rangle, l) \quad (St_0, En[\mathbf{v}(s) \mapsto x_1][\mathbf{v}(s') \mapsto 1]) \vdash e' \Rightarrow^E (St_1, v_1, l_1) \\
\ldots \quad (St_{m-1}, En[\mathbf{v}(s) \mapsto x_m][\mathbf{v}(s') \mapsto m]) \vdash e' \Rightarrow^E (St_m, v_m, l_m)
\end{array}
}{
(St, En) \vdash \mathtt{for\ } \$s \mathtt{\ at\ } \$s' \mathtt{\ in\ } e \mathtt{\ return\ } e' \Rightarrow^E (St_m, v_1 \circ \ldots \circ v_m, l \circ l_1 \circ \ldots \circ l_m)
}
$$

5 Expressive Power of Fragments of LiXQuery$^+$

In this section we compare the relative expressive power of a number of constructs of LiXQuery$^+$ by looking at different fragments of the language that do or do not contain these constructs.

5.1 LiXQuery$^+$ Fragments

The motivation for these fragments follows by their correspondence to existing query and update languages for XML, based on XQuery. In Section 6 we discuss the relation between these fragments and the existing update languages. First, we define the following four fragments of LiXQuery$^+$:

- The fragment XQ corresponds intuitively to non-recursive XQuery. More precisely, the non-terminals $\langle Insert\rangle$, $\langle Rename\rangle$, $\langle Replace\rangle$, $\langle Delete\rangle$, $\langle Snap\rangle$, and $\langle Transform\rangle$ are removed from LiXQuery$^+$, as well as $\langle FunDecl\rangle$.
- The fragment XQ_t corresponds to non-recursive XQuery extended with transformations. It is defined as LiXQuery$^+$ without $\langle Snap\rangle$ and $\langle FunDecl\rangle$ and where $\langle Insert\rangle$, $\langle Rename\rangle$, $\langle Replace\rangle$, and $\langle Delete\rangle$ only occurs within the body of the "modify" clause of a $\langle Transform\rangle$ expression.
- The fragment XQ_+ corresponds to non-recursive XQuery extended with the update operations, but without the $\langle Snap\rangle$ operation. It is defined as LiXQuery$^+$without $\langle Snap\rangle$ and $\langle FunDecl\rangle$.
- The fragment $XQ_!$ corresponds to non-recursive XQuery extended with updates and snap operations. It is defined as LiXQuery$^+$ without $\langle FunDecl\rangle$.

We can add (recursive) function definitions to all these fragments, which we denote by adding a superscript R to the name of the fragments.

5.2 Expressiveness Relations Between Fragments

It seems intuitive to say that two programs express the same update function if they map the same input stores to the same output stores. However, a program can make changes to the store that cannot be observed, since the modified nodes are not reachable through the result sequence of the program or through document calls. Therefore, we assume that the result store of a program does not contain nodes that are no longer reachable, since such nodes can be safely garbage collected. More precisely, the garbage collection is defined by the function Γ_v that, given a sequence v, maps a store St to a new store St' by removing all trees from St for which the root node is not in the range of δ_{St} and for which no node of the tree is in v.

We now define the query and update relations that correspond to LiXQuery$^+$ programs. Since programs can return sequences over another store than the input store, we only consider mappings from a store to a sequence of *atomic values* in this paper, i.e., we only look at queries that do not return nodes. The *query relation* of a LiXQuery$^+$ program p is the relation $\mathcal{R}_p^Q$ between stores St and sequences of *atomic values* v such that $(St, v) \in \mathcal{R}_p^Q \Leftrightarrow \exists St' : (St, (\emptyset, \emptyset, \emptyset, \bot)) \vdash p \Rightarrow (St', v)$. The *update relation* of a LiXQuery$^+$ program p is the relation $\mathcal{R}_p^U$ between stores St and St' such that $(St, St') \in \mathcal{R}_p^U \Leftrightarrow \exists St'', v : (St, (\emptyset, \emptyset, \emptyset, \bot)) \vdash p \Rightarrow (St'', v) \wedge \Gamma_v(St'') = St'$.

The following two partial orders are defined on LiXQuery$^+$ fragments:
- $XF_1 \succeq^Q XF_2$ iff $\forall p \in XF_2 : \exists p' \in XF_1 : \mathcal{R}_p^Q = \mathcal{R}_{p'}^Q$.
- $XF_1 \succeq^U XF_2$ iff $\forall p \in XF_2 : \exists p' \in XF_1 : \mathcal{R}_p^U = \mathcal{R}_{p'}^U$.

Based on these partial orders $\succeq^Q$ and $\succeq^U$ we define in the usual way the strict partial orders $\succ^Q$ and $\succ^U$, and the equivalence relations $\equiv^Q$ and $\equiv^U$ which are called *query-equivalence* and *update-equivalence*, respectively. Note that $XF_1 \not\equiv^Q XF_2 \Rightarrow XF_1 \not\equiv^U XF_2$, since we can translate in all fragments a result sequence of atomic values to a node containing a sequence of nodes that each contain one of the atomic values, and vice versa.

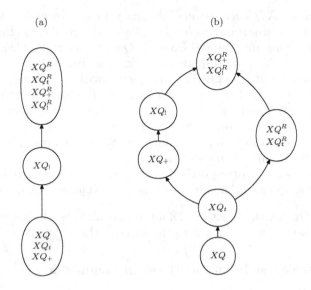

Fig. 3. Relations between the fragments in terms of expressive power of (a) mappings from stores to sequences of atomic values and (b) mappings from stores to stores

Theorem 1. *For the graph in part (a) of Fig. 3 and for all fragments XF_1, XF_2 it holds that $XF_1 \equiv^Q XF_2 \iff XF_1$ and XF_2 are within the same node, and $XF_1 \succ^Q XF_2 \iff$ there is a directed path from the node containing XF_2 to the node containing XF_1.*

Proof. (Sketch) This theorem will be proven in the remainder of this section. We now sketch which lemmas are needed to complete this proof. From Lemma 4 it follows that $XQ \equiv^Q XQ_t \equiv^Q XQ_+$, and from Lemma 2, Lemma 3, and Lemma 5 it follows that $XQ^R \equiv^Q XQ_t^R \equiv^Q XQ_+^R \equiv^Q XQ_!^R$. From Lemma 7 and Lemma 8 follows that $XQ_! \succ^Q XQ_+$ and from Lemma 9 follows that $XQ_!^R \succ^Q XQ_!$.

Theorem 2. *For the graph in part (b) of Fig. 3 and for all fragments XF_1, XF_2 it holds that $XF_1 \equiv^U XF_2 \iff XF_1$ and XF_2 are within the same node, and $XF_1 \succ^U XF_2 \iff$ there is a directed path from the node containing XF_2 to the node containing XF_1.*

Proof. (Sketch) This theorem will be proven in the remainder of this section. We now sketch which lemmas are needed to complete this proof. From Lemma 3 it follows that $XQ^R \equiv^U XQ_t^R$ and from Lemma 2 follows that $XQ_+^R \equiv^U XQ_!^R$. From Lemma 7 and Lemma 8 follows that $XQ_! \succ^U XQ_+$ and from Lemma 9 follows that $XQ_!^R \succ^U XQ_!$ and $XQ_!^R \succ^U XQ_t$. Moreover, we know by Lemma 6 that $XQ_+ \succ^U XQ_t$ and $XQ_+^R \succ^U XQ_t^R$. By Lemma 10 and Lemma 11 we get that $XQ_t \succ^U XQ$. Finally, it follows from Lemma 6 and Lemma 9 that $XQ_!$ and XQ_+ are incomparable with XQ^R.

5.3   Expressibility Results

In this subsection, we present the lemmas that are used to prove the query- or update-equivalence of LiXQuery$^+$ fragments.

Lemma 2. *For all $XQ_!^R$ programs p it holds that there is a XQ_+^R program p' that has the same update relation and the same query relation.*

Proof. (Sketch) In [8] we have shown that node construction in XQ^R does not add expressive power for "node-conservative deterministic queries". This was shown by encoding the store into a sequence of atomic values and simulating expressions with node construction to manipulate this encoded store. Using a similar simulation technique we can encode the output store, output sequence and list of pending updates in one sequence. Note that we have to use recursive functions to simulate the behavior of for-loops, since the encoded result store of one iteration has to be the input encoded store of the next iteration. Moreover, to ensure a correct computation, we have to apply updates on the encoded store as soon as they are applied in the $XQ_!^R$ expression. Note also that in the simulation we have to use node construction as source of non-determinism in order to have the same update relations. This can be done by expressions like (`element {"a"} {()}`) `<<` (`element {"a"} {()}`). Finally, we obtain the result store by performing the (encoded) lists of pending updates and performed updates in the correct order.

Lemma 3. *For all XQ_t^R programs p it holds that there is a XQ^R program p' that has the same update relation and the same query relation.*

Proof. (Sketch) We use the same simulation as sketched in the proof of Lemma 2. Since the nodes of the input store are not modified by transform-expressions, we only extend the input store. The result store can be obtained at the end of the simulation by using a recursive function that creates new nodes for nodes that are in the encoded output store but not in the input store.

Lemma 4. *For all XQ_+ programs p it holds that there is a XQ program p' that has the same query relation.*

Proof. (Sketch) Similar to the proof of Lemma 2 and Lemma 3 we can simulate all expressions to work on an encoded store. However, since we now do not have recursive functions to do the simulation, we have to keep track of the transitive closure of E, which we can obtain by using the descendant axis. It can be shown that all updates that are expressible in XQ_+ can be simulated, since we can express the corresponding updates on the encoded descendant relation in XQ.

Lemma 5. *For all $XQ_!^R$ programs p it holds that there is a XQ^R program p' that has the same query relation.*

Proof. (Sketch) The proof of this lemma is similar to that of Lemma 2 and Lemma 4. However, at the end we do not have to create the result store, but it suffices to return the result sequence, which only contains atomic values.

5.4   Inexpressibility Results

We now present the lemmas that are used to show that two LiXQuery$^+$ fragments are not query- or update-equivalent.

Lemma 6. *There are XQ_+ programs which have an update relation that we cannot express by a program in XQ_t^R.*

Proof. (Sketch) This can easily be seen by the fact that in XQ_+ we can modify nodes from the input store, while we cannot do this in XQ_t^R.

Lemma 7. *For all XQ_+ programs p it holds that the largest number (atomic value) in the output sequence is polynomially bounded by the number of nodes in the input store, the length of the longest sequence in the environment and the largest number (atomic value) in both the store and the environment.*

Proof. (Sketch) This can be shown by induction on the structure of the program. In [4] this was shown for the fragment that we refer to as XQ in this paper. From the simulation used to prove Lemma 4 it holds that the same polynomial upper bounds also holds for XQ_+ expressions, because the size of the simulating expression is polynomially bounded by the size of the simulated expression.

Lemma 8. *$XQ_!$ can express all primitive recursive functions over integers.*

Proof. (Sketch) We can give a translation that maps primitive recursive functions to $XQ_!$ expressions with one free variable, which models the arguments of such functions, i.e., tuples of natural numbers. It can easily be seen that the zero function, the succesor function, the projection and the composition can already be expressed in XQ. Primitive recursion can be simulated in $XQ_!$ by using the for-expression and the snap operation, which allows us to do bounded iteration.

Lemma 9. *There are programs in XQ^R which have a query relation that we cannot express by a program in $XQ_!$.*

Proof. (Sketch) It can be shown that all $XQ_!$ programs can be simulated by Turing machines that always halt, while XQ^R is Turing-complete.

Lemma 10. *For all XQ programs there is a depth d such that all nodes that are in the result store, but not in the input store and that have at least d ancestors are deep-equal to nodes in the input store.*

Proof. (Sketch) This property can be shown by induction on the structure of the program. Only node construction can create new nodes and the result is a new tree in the store, where all nodes except for the root are deep-equal to nodes that already existed, i.e., that are in the result store of the subexpression.

Lemma 11. *The property of Lemma 10 does not hold for XQ_t programs.*

Proof. (Sketch) This XQ_t program does not satisfy the property of Lemma 10:

```
transform copy $x := doc("a.xml") modify (for $y in $x//a return
rename $y as "b") return $x
```

6   Relation to Other XQuery-Based Update Languages

In this section we briefly discuss the relationship of various LiXQuery$^+$ fragments and a number of existing proposals that extend XQuery with updates.

The first proposal that we consider is UpdateX [10,1] which corresponds closely to XQ_+ and with XQ_+^R if recursive function definitions are allowed. They have a notion similar to a list of pending updates and the updates in this list are applied in the order that they are generated, as in XQ_+. The constructs of XQ_+ that are not in UpdateX include transform and rename operations. However, as can be seen from the proof of Lemma 4 it is possible to simulate programs that contain transform expressions with programs that do not.

The second proposal that we consider is XQuery! which is an extension of UpdateX with a snap operation. Hence it closely corresponds to $XQ_!$ and with $XQ_!^R$ if recursive function definitions are allowed. A small difference is that in UpdateX the semantics of the implicit top-level snap expressions is of the type *unordered deterministic*, a mode that they call *conflict-free*.

The final and third proposal that we consider is the XQuery Update Facility which corresponds closely to XQ_+ and with XQ_+^R if recursive function definitions are allowed. The semantics of this proposal differs in some details with the semantics of LiXQuery$^+$. For example, their semantics of the "replace value of" operation allows to change the content of element nodes, which can be simulated in LiXQuery$^+$. This proposal has an explicit "transform" operation, which the other two proposals lack but is included in XQ_+. An important difference is that at the time of writing the working draft does not allow to mix updating and non-updating expressions anymore, i.e., queries and updates are split. We propose that, as is demonstrated by the presented syntax and semantics of LiXQuery$^+$, it is straightforward to define the semantics of a language that does not have this restriction. Moreover, it can be shown that for all LiXQuery$^+$ programs p there exists an equivalent program p' where all queries and updates are split, i.e., there are no subexpressions that return both a non-empty result sequence and a non-empty list of pending updates. To prove this, we can use again a simulation of the store and list of pending updates, similar as used in the proof of Lemma 5. We can do this as follows. First we declare a variable as the encoded result of the simulating expression. Note that the simulating expression generates no real pending update list, only an encoded one. Then we extract and perform the encoded list of pending updates, and bind the resulting empty sequence to a variable. Finally, we can extract the result sequence from the encoded result sequence and return this as result of the program.

7   Conclusion

In order to investigate the relative expressive power of some special constructs that were introduced in XQuery-based update languages, we define LiXQuery$^+$ which combines these constructs. The syntax and semantics of this language is formally defined, demonstrating that this can be done in a concise and complete fashion. We compare several subsets of LiXQuery$^+$ in terms of queries and updates that can be expressed. One observation that is made is that the "snap" operation adds expressive power, even for expressing queries, because it allows the simulation of primitive recursive functions without using recursive function definitions. Another observation is that the "transform" operation allows the construction of new trees that would require recursion in XQuery.

In future research we intend to look at the relative expressive power of the different types of "snap" operations. Another subject of interest is finding better characterizations of the expressive power of the presented fragments. For example, we suspect that $XQ_!$ can express exactly all primitive recursive functions over XML trees.

References

1. M. Benedikt, A. Bonifati, S. Flesca, and A. Vyas. Adding updates to XQuery: Semantics, optimization, and static analysis. In *XIME-P*, 2005.
2. D. Chamberlin, D. Florescu, and J. Robie. XQuery update facility. W3C Working Draft, 2006. http://www.w3.org/TR/xqupdate/.
3. G. Ghelli, C. Ré, and J. Siméon. XQuery!: An XML query language with side effects. In *DataX 2006*, Munich, Germany, 2006.
4. J. Hidders, S. Marrara, J. Paredaens, and R. Vercammen. On the expressive power of XQuery fragments. In *DBPL 2005*, Trondheim, Norway, 2005.
5. J. Hidders, J. Paredaens, and R. Vercammen. Comparing the expressive power of XQuery-based update languages. Technical Report TR UA 2006-10, University of Antwerp, Dept. of Mathematics and Computer Science, 2006. http://adrem.ua.ac.be/pub/TR2006-10.pdf.
6. J. Hidders, J. Paredaens, and R. Vercammen. LiXQuery$^+$: an XQuery-based update language. Technical report, University of Antwerp, Dept. of Mathematics and Computer Science, 2006. http://adrem.ua.ac.be/pub/lixqueryplus.pdf.
7. J. Hidders, J. Paredaens, R. Vercammen, and S. Demeyer. A light but formal introduction to XQuery. In *XSym 2004*, Toronto, Canada, 2004.
8. W. Le Page, J. Hidders, P. Michiels, J. Paredaens, and R. Vercammen. On the expressive power of node construction in XQuery. In *WebDB 2005*, 2005.
9. D. Obasanjo and S. B. Navathe. A proposal for an XML data definition and manipulation language. In *Proc. of EEXTT 2002*, London, UK, 2003.
10. G. M. Sur, J. Hammer, and J. Siméon. UpdateX - an XQuery-based language for processing updates in XML. In *PLAN-X*, 2004.
11. I. Tatarinov, Z. G. Ives, A. Y. Halevy, and D. S. Weld. Updating XML. In *SIGMOD Conference*, 2001.

Efficient Incremental Validation of XML Documents After Composite Updates

Denilson Barbosa, Gregory Leighton, and Andrew Smith

University of Calgary, Calgary AB T2N 1N4, Canada
{denilson, gleighto, smithaj}@cs.ucalgary.ca

Abstract. We describe an efficient method for the incremental validation of XML documents after composite updates. We introduce the class
of Bounded-Edit (BE) DTDs and XML Schemas, and give a simple incremental revalidation algorithm that yields optimal performance for them,
in the sense that its time complexity is linear in the number of operations
in the update. We give extensive experimental results showing that our
algorithm exhibits excellent scalability. Finally, we provide a statistical
analysis of over 250 DTDs and XML Schema specifications found on the
Web, showing that over 99% of them are in fact in BE.

1 Introduction

Although originally designed for large-scale Web content publishing, XML has
become the preferred format for representing and exchanging semistructured
data [1], and is gaining popularity as an encoding format in standard office applications, such as text editors [7,13]. XML documents often refer to a *document
schema*, usually a Document Type Definition (DTD) [8] or an XML Schema
specification (XSD) [20], that defines the legal ways of arranging the markup
tags. A document is said to be *valid* with respect to a schema if its markup is
consistent with the specifications in that schema. Validity is an important property, as it specifies that the document is syntactically and structurally correct;
thus, validity must be preserved whenever the document is updated.

Checking whether a document is valid from scratch (i.e., static validation)
requires reading the entire document once [19]. However, in applications where
the XML document is too large (e.g., Web databases[1]) or where updates are
frequent (e.g., users editing office documents), scanning the entire document after every update becomes prohibitively slow. The *incremental* validation of a
valid document consists of checking whether an update results in another valid
document before the changes are made [3,4,6,11,16]. In essence, incremental validation consists of recording all steps during the static validation, and, whenever
possible, modifying these steps in response to updates.

---

[1] MEDLINE [14] is a 45GB bibliographic database about biomedical research and the
clinical sciences; and PIR-NREF [18] is an 18GB collection of protein sequence data
from several genome sequencing projects.

S. Amer-Yahia et al. (Eds.): XSym 2006, LNCS 4156, pp. 107–121, 2006.

In previous work [4], we discussed efficient methods for the incremental validation of XML documents after atomic updates. In particular, we described a large class of document schemas, called 1,2-*conflict free*, that accounts for most schemas used in practice and admits an incremental validation algorithm that runs in $O(\log n)$ time, where n is the size of the document. In this paper we discuss a generalization of that class in which incremental validation of a composite update with k atomic operations can be done in $O(k \log n)$ time. Moreover, we give a statistical analysis of over 26,000 content models, from over 250 DTDs and XSDs found on the Web, showing that our methods are applicable to over 99% of these content models.

Outline. The remainder of this paper is organized as follows. We discuss related work in Section 2, and introduce the background and notation used in the paper in Section 3. We present our incremental validation algorithm and the class of bounded-edit document schemas in Section 4. In Section 5, we provide a statistical analysis of over 250 DTDs and XSDs found on the Web, while in Section 6 we present an experimental analysis of our algorithm on XMark documents of varying sizes. Finally, we conclude in Section 7.

2   Related Work

The traditional model for incremental re-computation is to maintain some auxiliary information besides the data [17]; in this model, the *complexity per-update* is the complexity of recomputing both the result and the auxiliary data from the input, the update, the old result and auxiliary data. The *space complexity* is measured by the size of the auxiliary information only.

In the following, we assume that elements in the document are accessed through an indexed store kept on secondary memory, and that reading/writing individual elements takes *logarithmic* time (in the size of the document).

Papakonstantinou and Vianu[16] propose an incremental validation method that uses complex data structures and algorithms closely related to those in [4,17]. In that work, a separate balanced tree is used for storing the children of each element in the document. The space complexity of their method is $O(ns^2)$ for DTDs and $O(ns^4)$ for Specialized DTDs [15], where n is the size of the document and s is the size of its DTD/schema. (Specialized DTDs are an abstraction of XML Schema allowing instances of different specializations of the same type to occur in the content of the same element). Using these data structures, the per-update complexity of their incremental validation algorithms after a composite update with k operations is $O(k \log^2 n)$ for (fixed) DTDs, and $O(k \log^3 n)$ for Specialized DTDs.

We take a different approach, in that we use simple data structures that incur substantially smaller storage overhead, thus being more attractive from a system implementation point of view. Also, we focus on characterizing the classes of DTDs and schemas for which incremental validation can be done efficiently using those data structures. We use a single tree for storing the entire document, and the storage costs for auxiliary information in our approach are as follows. For DTDs, the space requirements are $O(n \log s)$ in general, and *constant* for Conflict-Free DTDs [4]; for Specialized DTDs, the space requirements are increased by a factor of $O(t^2 \log t)$, where t is the number of distinct element types in the schema. Finally, our incremental validation algorithms for composite updates require $O(n \log n)$ time in the worst case and $O(k \log n)$ time for bounded-edit (Section 4.2) DTDs and schemas.

3 Definitions

For the moment, we consider the problems of validation and incremental validation with respect to DTDs, we will discuss handling XSDs later. A DTD consists of sets of rules for specifying the types of elements and their attributes. An element specification rule assigns a *content model* to elements of a given *label*. Element specification rules constrain the structure of the document, by specifying the valid ways of nesting the elements in the document.

Let Σ be a set of element labels. Content models are given as 1-unambiguous regular expressions [9] of the form $E := \varepsilon \mid a \mid \#\text{PCDATA} \mid (E) \mid E|E \mid E, E \mid E* \mid E+ \mid E?$, where: ε is the empty string, $a \in \Sigma$, $\#\text{PCDATA}$ represents textual content, $E|E$ is the union operator, E, E is the concatenation operator, $E*$ is the usual Kleene star operator, and $E+$ and $E?$ are variations of the Kleene star that restrict the number of occurrences to at-least-one, and zero-or-one, respectively. That is, $E+ = E, E*$ and $E? = (E \mid \varepsilon)$.

Informally, a regular expression is 1-unambiguous if one can uniquely match an occurrence of a symbol in the regular expression to a character in the input string without looking beyond that character. That is, 1-unambiguous regular expressions require a lookahead of one symbol only.

We model DTDs as follows:

Definition 1 (Document Type Definition). *An XML Document Type Definition (DTD) is a triple $\langle \Sigma, r, \mathbf{R} \rangle$ where $r \in \Sigma$ is a distinguished label and $\mathbf{R}$ is a total function associating to each $a \in \Sigma$ a content model defined by a 1-unambiguous regular expression over $\Sigma \cup \{\#\text{PCDATA}\}$.*

One can test whether a regular expression E is 1-unambiguous by checking whether its corresponding Glushkov automaton [22] is deterministic [9]. First, we mark the symbols in E with subscripts to distinguish among different occurrences of the same symbol. For instance, a *marking* of the regular expression $a(b* \mid (c, b*))$ is $a(b_1* \mid (c, b_2*))$. E' denotes the marked version of E; each symbol in E' (subscripted or not) is called a *position* of E, denoted $pos(E)$. The subscripting is such that if $F \mid G$ or F, G are regular expressions, then $pos(F)$ and $pos(G)$ are disjoint. A marked regular expression E' is a regular expression over the alphabet $pos(E)$, such that each subscripted symbol occurs at most once in E'. Moreover, for each word w matched by a 1-unambiguous regular expression E, there is exactly one *marked word* w' in $L(E')$ that corresponds to w; also, w' can be constructed incrementally by examining the next symbol of w [9].

Notice that, by construction, in the Glushkov automaton of a regular expression E, states correspond to positions of E and transitions connect those

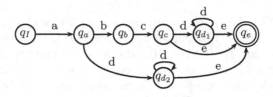

Fig. 1. Glushkov automaton of regular expression $E = a, ((b, c, d*) \mid d+), e$

positions that can be consecutive in a word in $L(E')$ [22]. We will exploit this property later for characterizing different kinds of XML content models.

Figure 1 shows the transition diagram of the Glushkov automaton for the 1-unambiguous regular expression $E = a, ((b, c, d*) \mid d+), e$.

3.1   Element and Document Validity

An element e is said to be *valid* if its content (i.e., the sequence of elements and text nodes that are children of e) conforms with the content model associated with its type. More precisely, let D be a document, e be an element in D, and $\mathcal{D} = \langle \Sigma, r, \mathbf{R} \rangle$ be a DTD. The *content string* of e is formed by the concatenation of the labels of all nodes in its content, ignoring attributes (text nodes are labeled PCDATA). We say e is valid with respect to $\mathcal{D}$ if its content string w is a word matched by the content model associated with its label in $\mathbf{R}$. Also, we say that D is valid with respect to $\mathcal{D}$, denoted $D \in L(\mathcal{D})$, if all its elements are valid with respect to $\mathcal{D}$ and the label of its root element is r.

Notice that every symbol in the content string of an element e corresponds to a single element or text node forming e's content. Thus we will use the terms element content and content string interchangeably from now on.

Incremental Validation. We refer to *static* validation as the process of determining whether a document is valid with respect to its DTD. In a dynamic scenario where updates are applied, it is necessary to prevent updates to a valid document that result in invalid ones. The *incremental validation* problem is defined as: given $D \in L(\mathcal{D})$, and an update U, is it the case that $U(D) \in L(\mathcal{D})$?

3.2   XML Updates

In this work, we consider a minimal set of low-level update primitives that could be used for implementing update expressions given in a high-level update language (e.g., see [10]), or used directly by an XML editor.

Each primitive consists of an *atomic* operation, informally defined as follows. Let D be an XML document, x be the identifier of an element in D, and y be a constant describing an element not in D. An *Append*(x, y) applied to D appends y as the last child of the element pointed to by x. An *InsertBefore*(x, y) applied to D inserts y as the immediate left sibling of the element pointed to by x. Finally, *Delete*(x) applied to D removes from D the element pointed to by x.

Name	Type	Search Key	Data	Unique?
Edge	B-tree	`element_id`	`parent_id, type, state`	Yes
LS	B-tree	`element_id`	`id_left`	Yes
RS	B-tree	`element_id`	`id_right`	Yes
FLC	B-tree	`element_id`	`id_first, id_last`	Yes
Transition	B-tree	`parent_type, from`	`to, type, label`	No
Content	Hash file	`element_id`	`pcdata_value`	Yes

Fig. 2. Main data structures for storing XML documents. The **Search Key** column indicates the values used as index keys for accessing the associated data; the column **Unique** determines whether the keys are unique for each entry.

We also allow *composite* update operations, which consist of an ordered sequence of one or more of the primitive operations above. Without loss of generality, we assume that each composite update modifies the content of a single element in the document. Also, we assume that in a composite update all *InsertBefore*$(\cdot,\cdot)$ and *Delete*$(\cdot)$ operations precede all *Append*$(\cdot,\cdot)$ operations. Finally, we assume that if an *InsertBefore*(x_1, y) precedes a *Delete*(x_2) then either $x_1 = x_2$ or the element pointed to by x_1 precedes the element pointed to by x_2 in the document. In other words, the primitive operations in a composite update are sorted according to the relative position of the elements they modify. We will come back to this assumption later on.

Notice that one can construct any XML document with these three primitives, and more complex operations (e.g., copying elements) can be rewritten as sequences of them.

3.3   Storage Data Structures

We use the data structures described in Figure 2 for storing the XML documents in our approach. For simplicity, we ignore XML attributes (see [4] for a discussion of how to handle the incremental validation of attribute constraints in our work). The Edge file materializes the parent-child relationship among elements and also between elements and text nodes. The textual (PCDATA) content of element nodes is kept in the Content file. The LS (for left-sibling) and RS (resp. right-sibling) files materialize the predecessor and successor relations among sibling elements, respectively; the FLC file keeps track of the first and last children of every non-empty element in the document. Finally, the Transition file stores the transition functions of all content models in the DTD; different content models are identified by the `parent_type` component of the search key for that file.

In this work, we assume that the access and update cost for each file above to be logarithmic in the size of the document.

4   Efficient Incremental Validation

In this section we give a general algorithm for the incremental validation of XML documents w.r.t. DTDs after composite updates (Section 4.1), describe a class

> function **findTransition**(q, l)
> $\quad q' \leftarrow \delta(q, l)$
> $\quad$ if $[q'$ is undefined$]$ then **reject** else return q'
>
> function **findStartingState**(u)
> $\quad$ if $[eid(u)$ is first child$]$ then $q \leftarrow q_I$
> $\quad$ else $x \leftarrow eid(u) - 1;\ q \leftarrow state(x)$ fi
> $\quad$ return q
>
> function **readOld**(q, x, y)
> $\quad$ do $q' \leftarrow$ findTransition$(q, label(x));\ x \leftarrow rightSibling(x)$
> $\quad$ while $[q' \neq state(y)$ and x has a right sibling and $x \neq y]$
> $\quad$ return (q', y)

Fig. 3. Helper procedures for the incremental validation algorithm

of DTDs for which this algorithm has a much better worst-case time complexity than full revalidation from scratch (Section 4.2), and discuss ways of actually effecting the updates (Section 4.3).

The setting is as follows. Let e be an element, $w = w_1 \ldots w_n$ be its content string, E be the 1-unambiguous regular expression defining the content model of e, $G = (Q, \Sigma, \delta, q_I, F)$ be the Glushkov automaton of E, and $U = u_1, \ldots, u_k$ be a composite update with k primitive operations. Initially e is valid; i.e., $w \in L(G)$. We want to determine whether $U(w) \in L(G)$, using an auxiliary data structure containing the path of w through G (i.e., the sequence $\tilde{w} = q_I q_1 \ldots q_n$, where each $q_i \in Q$, $i > 0$ is the state in G we reach after reading w_i). We assume that $k \ll n$. (Recall n is the size of the document.)

4.1   Algorithm

For the sake of readability, we introduce the following notation. We will denote by $eid(u)$ the element id specified by an update operation u; that is, if $u = InsertBefore(x, \cdot)$ then $eid(u) = x$, and if $u = Delete(x)$, then $eid(u) = x$. We denote by $rightSibling(x)$ the element id of the immediate right sibling of the element pointed to by x. We will use $label(x)$ to denote the label of an element with id x already in the document. If u is an $InsertBefore(\cdot, y)$ or $Append(\cdot, y)$ operation, we denote by $label(u)$ the the label of the element y. Finally, we denote by $state(x)$ the DFA state associated with element x during the static validation.

Figure 3 shows some procedures which are used in the main algorithm, given in Figure 4. The algorithm works in two separate phases: first we deal with all $InsertBefore(\cdot, \cdot)$ and $Delete(\cdot)$ operations (lines 2-22); then we deal with $Append(\cdot, \cdot)$ operations (lines 23-27). We discuss each separately next.

Insertions and Deletions. Because of the way the update operations are ordered (recall Section 3.2), the incremental validation of insertions and deletions can be done by simultaneously scanning the content string w and $u_1, \ldots, u_k$ once. In

Input: composite update $u_1, \ldots, u_k$

1. *restart* ← true; $i \leftarrow 1$
2. while [$i < k$ and u_i is not an append] do
3.   if [*restart*] then *restart* ← false; *from* ← findStartingState(u_i) fi
4.   if [u_i is a deletion] then
5.   do *rs* ← *rightSibling*($eid(u_i)$); $i \leftarrow i + 1$;
6.   while [u_i is a deletion and $eid(u_i) = rs$]
7.   if [$eid(u_{i-1})$ was last child] then
8.   if [*from* $\notin F$] then reject else continue fi
9.   fi
10. (to, ce) ← readOld(*from*, *rs*, $eid(u_i)$)
11.   if [*ce* is last child and *to* $\notin F$] then reject fi
12.   if [$eid(u_{i+1}) \neq ce$] then *restart* ← true fi
13.   *from* ← *to*; continue
14.   fi
15.   if [u_i is an insertion] then
16.   do *to* ← findTransition(*from*, label(u_i)); *from* ← *to*; $i \leftarrow i + 1$
17.   while [u_i is an insertion and $eid(u_i) = eid(u_{i-1})$]
18.   *rs* ← *rightSibling*($eid(u_{i-1})$); (to, ce) ← readOld(*from*, *rs*, $eid(u_i)$)
19.   if [*ce* is last child and *to* $\notin F$] then reject fi
20.   if [$eid(u_{i+1}) \neq ce$] then *restart* ← true fi
21.   fi
22. endwhile
23. if [$i < k$] then
24.   let *from* be the state of the last child of the element being updated
25.   do *to* ← findTransition(*from*, label(u_i)); *from* ← *to*; $i \leftarrow i + 1$ while [$i \leq k$]
26.   if [*to* $\notin F$] then reject fi
27. fi
28. accept

Fig. 4. Algorithm for the incremental validation of a composite update operation. F denotes the set of accepting states for the Glushkov automaton corresponding to the content model of the element being modified.

the algorithm of Figure 4, *from* keeps the current state during the revalidation process, and u_i refers to the current atomic operation being executed. Notice that *from* is initialized by the function findStartingState($\cdot$) (see Figure 3) as follows. If the current operation u_i refers to the first child of e (the element being updated), *from* is set to the initial state q_I. On the other hand, if $eid(u_i)$ is not the first child of e, we start revalidating from the state of its immediate left sibling, which is kept in the auxiliary data structure.

The revalidation after the deletion of one or more consecutive elements consists of simply "skipping" all symbols in w that correspond to elements being deleted (lines 5-6 in Figure 4) and simulating the DFA from the *from* state, reading the remaining symbols in w (line 10). This revalidation continues until one of these conditions is met: (a) we simulate one step in the DFA and arrive at the same state in $\tilde{w}$ for the corresponding element; (b) we reach an element

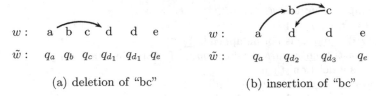

(a) deletion of "bc"   (b) insertion of "bc"

Fig. 5. Revalidation after deletion (a) and insertion (b), using the DFA from Figure 1. The arrows indicate the new transitions that must be computed.

that will be affected by the next update operation; or (c) we reach the end of w, in which case we reject the update if the current state is not an accepting one.

In cases (a) and (b) we continue the revalidation by jumping to the next update operation; the difference between the two cases is that in (b) we have to find a new value for the *from* variable.

The revalidation after two consecutive deletions is illustrated by Figure 5(a). In the figure, $w = abcdde$ ($\tilde{w} = q_a q_b q_c q_{d_1} q_{d_1} q_e$) and the update consists of deleting the substring "bc"; in this case, we must find a transition from q_a labeled with d, as indicated by the arrow. Because $\delta(q_a, d) = q_{d_2}$, which is different than the state previously associated with that symbol in $\tilde{w}$, we continue revalidating w (until we reach the last symbol e, in this case).

The revalidation of insertion operations is very similar to that of deletion operations. The only difference is that instead of "skipping" the labels of elements being deleted we simulate the DFA using the labels of those elements being inserted at the same position in w (lines 16-17). Once all new element labels are "consumed", we continue the revalidation using the elements already in the document, as illustrated by Figure 5(b). The same conditions for stopping the revalidation as in the deletion case apply here.

Appends. Handling the *Append*($\cdot, \cdot$) operations (lines 23-27 in Figure 4) is straightforward. All that needs to be done is finding the state of the last child of the element being updated (line 24), and simulating the DFA using the labels of the elements being appended. We accept only if we reach an accepting state after consuming all symbols being appended.

Putting it all Together. In summary, the revalidation of an arbitrary composite update $u_1, \ldots, u_k$ consists of simultaneously scanning the list of updates and the element being modified, alternating between deletions and insertions as outlined above, and applying all appends at the very end. Next, we will discuss the complexity of this algorithm for arbitrary DTDs, and characterize one class of DTDs for which the algorithm is guaranteed to perform well in practice.

Analysis of the Algorithm. We now discuss the correctness and the computational complexity of our algorithm. The following is easy to verify:

Proposition 1. *If s is the content string resulting from applying the composite update defined by $u_1, \ldots, u_k$ over the content of a valid element e, then $s \in L(G)$ if and only if the algorithm in Figure 4 accepts on input $u_1, \ldots, u_k$.*

The complexity of our algorithm is as follows. The loop for insertions and deletions (lines 2-22) runs $O(k)$ times, inserting or deleting elements. Revalidation after a single insertion or deletion may require revalidating all of the original content string in the worst case. However, notice that because of the way the operations are sorted and the fact that the algorithm never uses an element that is to the left of the one being considered, the loop of lines 2-22 never scans the same element twice. Similarly, the loop for handling appends (lines 23-27) runs in $O(k)$ time. Notice also that all document operations in the algorithm consist of finding the right sibling, the parent or the ids of the first and last children of an element, all of which require $O(\log n)$ time using our data structures. Thus, the incremental validation of a composite update can be done in $O((k + n) \log n) = O(n \log n)$ time.

The only auxiliary information used by the algorithm is the path $\tilde{w}$ of the content string w through the Glushkov automaton, computed during the static validation of the document. Storing such data requires $O(n \log d)$ space, where $d = O(|\mathcal{D}|)$ and $\mathcal{D}$ is the DTD used for validating the document.

As we can see, the worst case complexity of the incremental validation algorithm above, as expected, matches that of full revalidation from scratch. The reason for this is, as in the case of processing each atomic update at a time [4], we might have to revalidate the entire content string.

Ordering Atomic Updates. We now revisit our initial assumption that the atomic operations in a composite update are sorted according to the *relative position* of the elements they refer to (recall Section 3.2), which is central to the efficiency of our algorithm. Notice that this causes no problem in the setting of an XML editor, in which case the XML document being edited is already in memory, thus allowing the editor to keep track of the relative ordering of elements. A more challenging scenario is that of an XML database being updated by means of a declarative language. In this setting, one would use predicates (e.g., XPath expressions) for selecting the nodes defining the positions in the content string that are affected by the update. Thus, we need a way of ordering two nodes e_1 and e_2 (i.e., knowing which comes *before* the other) given just their ids . One way of accomplishing this is to materialize the transitive closure of the successor relation among siblings (recall Section 3.3), and maintain it after updates—which can be done efficiently [12].

While the previous approach is viable, a simpler method that would suffice here is to keep the position of every element relative to its siblings, and a counter that indicates the *age* of that element. Notice that the relative ordering of nodes e_1 and e_2 is not affected by deletions of other nodes; also, the relative ordering can be easily maintained after appends (because we can always find the ordering of the last element); thus, the only concern is the *InsertBefore*$(\cdot, \cdot)$ operation. Let e be an element whose relative ordering is o, and whose age is a; when we insert $y_1, \ldots, y_k$ before e, for each y_i, we define its ordering as $o - 1 + i$, and its age $a + 1$. Thus, it follows that e_1 precedes e_2 if either e_1's ordering is less than that of e_2 *or* e_1 is newer than e_2. Notice that using this simple scheme does not change the time complexity of our algorithm.

Type Specialization. Throughout the paper our discussion centered around DTDs only. As mentioned earlier, our method also applies to some aspects of XML Schema, namely *type specialization*, which allows different content models to be assigned to elements with the same label, depending on the *context* in which they appear [20]. As discussed in detail in [4], this can be accomplished by adding another column to the search key of the Transition file (recall Section 3.3) for keeping track of the element context. Because of the way XML Schema defines type specialization, every element *type* defines a new context.

4.2   Bounded-Edit DTDs

We now define a class of DTDs that admit much more efficient incremental validation for composite updates. To motivate the discussion, consider again the content model $E = a, ((b, c, d*) \mid d+), e$, whose Glushkov automaton is given in Figure 1, and the string $w = abcdd \cdots de$, where all d symbols match position d_1. A composite update that deletes "bc" from w causes all d elements to match d_2 instead of d_1 as before. That is, the incremental validation of this update requires $O(n)$ ($n = |w|$) steps (and changes to $\tilde{w}$ as well), which is undesirable.

Intuitively, we want DTDs in which the amount of work required for the incremental validation of an element is independent of the length of its content string (and thus, is independent of the document size). That is, the amount of revalidation work for such DTDs is bounded by inherent properties of the content models in them.

Recall that the *edit distance* between two strings is the minimum number of character insertions and/or deletions that make the two strings identical [2]. We define the following:

Definition 2 (Bounded-Edit DTDs). *E is a* bounded-edit *regular expression if E is 1-unambiguous and there exists $l > 0$ that depends on E and such that for every composite update $u_1, \ldots, u_k$ and $w \in L(E)$ we have that if $s = U(w)$ and $s \in L(E)$ then the edit distance between the marked versions of w and s is at most $k + l$.*

A DTD $\mathcal{D} = \langle \Sigma, r, \mathbf{R} \rangle$ is bounded-edit *(BE) if all regular expressions defining content models in $\mathbf{R}$ are bounded-edit.*

Notice that the number of steps needed by the algorithm in Figure 4 to determine whether $s = U(w) \in L(E)$ is bounded by the edit distance between w' and s'. Thus, the following is immediate:

Corollary 1. *The incremental validation of a composite update with k atomic operations for a bounded-edit DTD $\mathcal{D}$ can be done in $O((k+l) \log n)$ time, where l depends on $\mathcal{D}$ only.*

We now give a characterization of BE regular expressions (and thus DTDs) based on structural properties of their Glushkov automata.

Proposition 2. *Let E be a regular expression and G its Glushkov automaton. E is bounded-edit if and only if G does not have two disjoint sets of states*

$x_1, \ldots, x_m$ and $y_1, \ldots, y_m$ such that: x_1 and y_1 are reachable from q_I; x_i and y_i, $1 \leq i \leq m$, correspond to positions of the same unmarked symbol; and both $x_1, x_2, \ldots, x_m, x_1$ and $y_1, y_2, \ldots, y_m, y_1$ spell cycles through G.

For instance, $E = a, ((b, c, d*) \mid d+), e$ is not BE because $\{q_{d_1}\}$ and $\{q_{d_2}\}$ satisfy all the conditions specified in Proposition 2.

4.3   Effecting the Updates

The algorithm in Figure 4 deals with checking whether the composite update is permissible. We now consider effecting the changes after an update is deemed permissible.

Updating both the content string w and its path through G ($\tilde{w}$) requires (asymptotically) the same time as determining whether the update is permissible, since our algorithms visit only those symbols in w and $\tilde{w}$ that must be visited for the incremental validation. Three basic strategies are possible for effecting the changes: (1) buffering the results of the incremental validation first, and effecting them if the update is deemed permissible; (2) making a second pass over the string for effecting the changes if the update is deemed permissible; or (3) effecting the changes during the revalidation, undoing them if the update is deemed not permissible. For simplicity, we use the latter approach, which can be easily implemented using transactions.

5   Statistical Analysis of Document Schemas

In this section, we present a statistical analysis of the content models found in several document schemas on the Web. We analyzed a sample consisting of 264 document schemas, containing both DTDs and XSDs. Among those, 92 DTDs and 59 XSDs in our sample were used in a previous statistical study of document schemas on the Web (Bex et al. [5]). The remaining schemas were collected from the xml.org repository. Collectively, these schemas account for 26604 content models; a very small number of those (14) were not 1-unambiguous, and thus were discarded.

We classify the content models in our sample according to the following categories: **simple** models define regular expressions of the form $r = r_1, \ldots, r_j$ where each $r_i = a \mid a* \mid a+ \mid a?$, a is an element label, and each label appears at most once in r; **CF** models allow arbitrary regular expressions in which each element label appears at most once [4]; **1,2-CF** models allow regular expressions in which there may be many occurrences of the same element label, provided they are not too close to each other [4]; **BE** is as defined in Section 4.2; **1-UNAM** models allow any 1-unambiguous regular expressions. Notice that

$$\text{simple} \subset \textbf{CF} \subset \textbf{1,2-CF} \subset \textbf{BE} \subset \textbf{1-UNAM}.$$

Testing whether a content model belongs to one of the classes above is done by a graph-traversal algorithm that checks whether the corresponding Glushkov

Table 1. Prevalence of content models in a sample of schemas found on the Web

Collection	simple	CF	1,2-CF	BE	1-UNAM	total
Counts						
DTDs from `xml.org`	15230	887	3	52	8	16180
DTDs from [5]	5569	1958	16	55	64	7662
XSDs from [5]	2551	204	1	6	0	2761
Percentages						
DTDs from `xml.org`	94.2%	5.5%	0.02%	0.32%	0.05%	100%
DTDs from [5]	72.7%	25.5%	0.24%	0.72%	0.84%	100%
XSDs from [5]	92.4%	7.4%	0.03%	0.20%	0%	100%

automaton satisfies the structural restrictions associated with each such class. Since XSDs are not defined directly in terms of regular expressions, we use the method of Bex et al. [5] for extracting the corresponding content models.

Table 1 shows the number of content models in each class above. The top half of the table shows absolute counts of content models in each class, while the bottom half shows the respective fractions relative to the total number of content models in the collection. For easier reading, we count each content model in the *most restrictive* class it belongs to. As one can see, the vast majority of content models in our sample are either CF (98% or more of them) or BE (99% or more). It should be noted that CF content models allow the same incremental validation algorithms to be implemented *without* the need for auxiliary space [4].

6   Experimental Evaluation

To evaluate the efficiency of our proposed incremental validation algorithm, we conducted two experiments on several synthetic XML documents generated according to the XMark benchmark specification [21]. The sizes of these documents were 512 KB, 4 MB, 32 MB, 256 MB, and 2 GB. Because the XMark DTD does not allow for composite updates involving more than one element type, we introduced two minor modifications to the content model of the `item` elements for the purposes of our tests; Figure 6 depicts these changes. We note that the modified XMark DTD is a bounded-edit schema. We implemented the algorithm using Berkeley DB to store the various data structures associated with our approach. While we conducted experiments with varying buffer sizes for the Berkeley DB engine, due to the lack of space we discuss here only those experiments in which the buffer size was capped at 128 KB. All experiments were executed on an desktop-class machine: Intel Pentium4 3.4 GHz processor, with 1 GB of RAM and running Linux 2.6.9. Finally, each plot in the graphs below represents the average over a number of trials (20 in the case of the 512 KB document, 50 for the remaining four documents), with outliers removed.

The first experiment was designed to simulate a localized editing operation; in order to do this, we pick an `item` element in the North America region at

```
<!ELEMENT item (location,quantity,..., payment,description,shipping,...>
```
(a) Original content model for item

```
<!ELEMENT item ((location | (number,street,zip,country)), quantity,...,
         ((payment, description, shipping)* | (delivery*)),...>
```
(b) Modified content model for item

Fig. 6. Modifications made to the XMark DTD for the purposes of our experiments

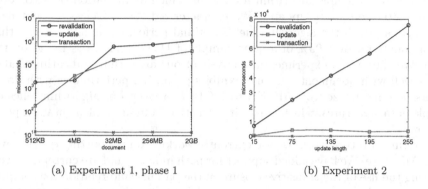

(a) Experiment 1, phase 1   (b) Experiment 2

Fig. 7. Experimental results. All times are reported in microseconds; notice the graph in (a) is shown in log-log scale.

random, and proceed as follows. In the first phase of the experiment, we applied a composite update operation that replaced the location of that item by a sequence consisting of a number, street, zip and a country element. Figure 7(a) shows the average times for revalidating the document, updating the document, and managing the transaction. The second phase consisted of essentially undoing the changes made in the first phase: the previously-inserted number, street, zip and country child elements of item were deleted and a location child element was inserted. (Due to the lack of space, we omit the graph for the second phase; the results provide a similar analysis to that of phase 1.) As one can see, update and revalidation times both exhibit excellent scalability with respect to document size, while the transaction overhead remains constant and negligible. Notice that the revalidation costs are virtually identical for the 512KB and 4MB documents; this is due to buffering done by Berkeley DB.

The second experiment measured the revalidation costs as a function of the *length* of the composite update (i.e., the number of atomic operations in it). For this experiment, we used the 32 MB XML document; each run of the experiment applied a composite update operation consisting of the deletion of the payment, description, and shipping child elements of a randomly-selected item in the North America region, followed by the insertion of a parameterized number of delivery elements as children of the item element. Figure 7(b) shows the results of this experiment using composite update operations in which 15, 75, 135, 195, and 255 delivery elements were inserted. Notice that, as expected, the revalidation time, which dominates the cost, increases linearly with the length of the update. The low (and almost constant) cost of updating the document is explained by the fact that not all update operations incur the creation of new pages on disk.

7   Conclusion

We presented a simple algorithm for the incremental validation of XML documents after composite updates. We characterized the BE class of document schemas for which the algorithm yields optimal performance, and showed that BE accounts for over 99% of a large sample of DTDs and XSDs found on the Web. We showed an experimental analysis of our algorithm, indicating that it scales well with document size, and exhibits promising performance with documents ranging in size from 512 KB to 2 GB. Moreover, our algorithm relies on simple data structures, which makes it attractive from an implementation point of view.

In terms of future work, we are currently working on supporting queries over our XML store. We have added support for path indexes, and are currently investigating the use of the transitive closure of the parent-child relation for computing ancestor-descendant queries efficiently. We believe that our data structures, coupled with indexes, can be used by a native XML store to provide efficient query and update processing. We also believe that, as the problems related to updating XML receive increased attention, a new generation of XML benchmarks will be needed.

Acknowledgments. The authors would like to thank Anastasios Kementsietsidis for providing code used in the analysis of the content models, and Jin Tao for helping in the implementation of the prototype. This work was supported in part by a grant from the Natural Sciences and Engineering Research Council of Canada. D. Barbosa is an Ingenuity New Faculty.

References

1. S. Abiteboul, P. Buneman, and D. Suciu. *Data on the Web*. Morgan Kauffman, 1999.
2. R. Baeza-Yates and B. Ribeiro-Neto. *Modern Information Retrieval*. Addison Wesley, 1999.
3. A. Balmin, Y. Papakonstantinou, and V. Vianu. Incremental Validation of XML Documents. *ACM Transactions on Database Systems*, 29(4):710–751, December 2004. Extended version of [16].
4. D. Barbosa, A. O. Mendelzon, L. Libkin, L. Mignet, and M. Arenas. Efficient Incremental Validation of XML Documents. In *Proceedings of the 20th International Conference on Data Engineering*, pages 671–682, Boston, MA, USA, 2004. IEEE Computer Society.

5. G. J. Bex, F. Neven, and J. V. den Bussche. DTDs versus XML Schema: A Practical Study. In *Proceedings of the Seventh International Workshop on the Web and Databases, WebDB 2004*, pages 79–84, Maison de la Chimie, Paris, France, June 17-18 2004.

6. B. Bouchou and M. Halfeld-Ferrari-Alvez. Updates and Incremental Validation of XML Documents. In *9th International Workshop on Database Programming Languages*, pages 216–232, Potsdam, Germany, September 6-8 2003.

7. M. Brauer, P. Durusau, G. Edwards, D. Faure, T. Magliery, and D. Vogelheim. Open Document Format for Office Applications (OpenDocument) v1.0. OASIS standard, Organization for the Advancement of Structured Information Standards (OASIS), 1 May 2005.

8. T. Bray, J. Paoli, C. M. Sperberg-McQueen, E. Maler, and F. Yergeau. *Extensible Markup Language (XML) 1.0*. World Wide Web Consortium, third edition, February 4 2004. http://www.w3.org/TR/2004/REC-xml-20040204.

9. A. Brüggemann-Klein and D. Wood. One-Unambiguous Regular Languages. *Information and Computation*, 142:182–206, 1998.

10. D. Chamberlin, D. Florescu, and J. Robie. XQuery Update Facility. W3C Working Draft, 8 May 2006.

11. B. Kane, H. Su, and E. A. Rundensteiner. Consistently Updating XML Documents Using Incremental Constraint Check Queries. In *Fourth ACM CIKM International Workshop on Web Information and Data Management*, pages 1–8, McLean, Virginia, USA, November 8 2002.

12. L. Libkin and L. Wong. On the Power of Incremental Evaluation in SQL-Like Languages. In *Proceedings of the 7th International Workshop on Database Programming Languages, DBPL'99*, pages 17–30, Kinloch Rannoch, Scotland, UK, September 1-3 1999.

13. Office 2003 XML Reference Schema. http://www.microsoft.com/office/xml, 2006.

14. National Library of Medicine, 2004. http://www.nlm.nih.gov/.

15. Y. Papakonstantinou and V. Vianu. DTD Inference for Views of XML Data. In *Proceedings of the 19th ACM SIGMOD-SIGACT-SIGART Symposium on Principles of Database Systems*, pages 35–46, May 15-18 2000.

16. Y. Papakonstantinou and V. Vianu. Incremental Validation of XML Documents. In D. Calvanese, M. Lenzerini, and R. Motwani, editors, *Proceeedings of The 9th International Conference on Database Theory*, number 2572 in Lecture Notes in Computer Science, pages 47–63, Siena, Italy, January 8-10 2003. Springer-Verlag.

17. S. Patnaik and N. Immerman. Dyn-FO: A Parallel, Dynamic Complexity Class. *J. Comput. Syst. Sci.*, 55(2):199–209, October 1997.

18. PIR Non-Redundant Reference Sequence Database (PIR-NREF), October 14 2004. http://pir.georgetown.edu/pirwww/search/pirnref.shtml.

19. L. Segoufin. Typing and Querying XML Documents: Some Complexity Bounds. In *Proceedings of the 22nd ACM SIGMOD-SIGACT-SIGART Symposium on Principles of Database Systems*, pages 167–178, San Diego, CA, USA, June 9-11 2003.

20. H. S. Thompson, D. Beech, M. Maloney, and N. M. (Editors). *XML Schema Part 1: Structures*. World Wide Web Consortium, May 2 2001. http://www.w3.org/TR/2001/REC-xmlschema-1-20010502/.

21. The XML benchmark project. http://www.xml-benchmark.org/.

22. S. Yu. Regular Languages. In G. Rozenberg and A. Saloma, editors, *Handbook of Formal Languages*, volume 1, pages 41–110. Springer, 1997.

Author Index

Lecture Notes in Computer Science

For information about Vols. 1–4060

please contact your bookseller or Springer

Vol. 4110: J. Díaz, K. Jansen, J.D.P. Rolim, U. Zwick (Eds.), Approximation, Randomization, and Combinatorial Optimization. XII, 522 pages. 2006.

Vol. 4109: D.-Y. Yeung, J.T. Kwok, A. Fred, F. Roli, D. de Ridder (Eds.), Structural, Syntactic, and Statistical Pattern Recognition. XXI, 939 pages. 2006.

Vol. 4108: J.M. Borwein, W.M. Farmer (Eds.), Mathematical Knowledge Management. VIII, 295 pages. 2006. (Sublibrary LNAI).

Vol. 4106: T.R. Roth-Berghofer, M.H. Göker, H. A. Güvenir (Eds.), Advances in Case-Based Reasoning. XIV, 566 pages. 2006. (Sublibrary LNAI).

Vol. 4104: T. Kunz, S.S. Ravi (Eds.), Ad-Hoc, Mobile, and Wireless Networks. XII, 474 pages. 2006.

Vol. 4099: Q. Yang, G. Webb (Eds.), PRICAI 2006: Trends in Artificial Intelligence. XXVIII, 1263 pages. 2006. (Sublibrary LNAI).

Vol. 4098: F. Pfenning (Ed.), Term Rewriting and Applications. XIII, 415 pages. 2006.

Vol. 4097: X. Zhou, O. Sokolsky, L. Yan, E.-S. Jung, Z. Shao, Y. Mu, D.C. Lee, D. Kim, Y.-S. Jeong, C.-Z. Xu (Eds.), Emerging Directions in Embedded and Ubiquitous Computing. XXVII, 1034 pages. 2006.

Vol. 4096: E. Sha, S.-K. Han, C.-Z. Xu, M.H. Kim, L.T. Yang, B. Xiao (Eds.), Embedded and Ubiquitous Computing. XXIV, 1170 pages. 2006.

Vol. 4095: S. Nolfi, G. Baldassare, R. Calabretta, D. Marocco, D. Parisi, J.C. T. Hallam, O. Miglino, J.-A. Meyer (Eds.), From Animals to Animats 9. XV, 869 pages. 2006. (Sublibrary LNAI).

Vol. 4094: O. H. Ibarra, H.-C. Yen (Eds.), Implementation and Application of Automata. XIII, 291 pages. 2006.

Vol. 4093: X. Li, O.R. Zaïane, Z. Li (Eds.), Advanced Data Mining and Applications. XXI, 1110 pages. 2006. (Sublibrary LNAI).

Vol. 4092: J. Lang, F. Lin, J. Wang (Eds.), Knowledge Science, Engineering and Management. XV, 664 pages. 2006. (Sublibrary LNAI).

Vol. 4091: G.-Z. Yang, T. Jiang, D. Shen, L. Gu, J. Yang (Eds.), Medical Imaging and Augmented Reality. XIII, 399 pages. 2006.

Vol. 4090: S. Spaccapietra, K. Aberer, P. Cudré-Mauroux (Eds.), Journal on Data Semantics VI. XI, 211 pages. 2006.

Vol. 4089: W. Löwe, M. Südholt (Eds.), Software Composition. X, 339 pages. 2006.

Vol. 4088: Z.-Z. Shi, R. Sadananda (Eds.), Agent Computing and Multi-Agent Systems. XVII, 827 pages. 2006. (Sublibrary LNAI).

Vol. 4087: F. Schwenker, S. Marinai (Eds.), Artificial Neural Networks in Pattern Recognition. IX, 299 pages. 2006. (Sublibrary LNAI).

Vol. 4085: J. Misra, T. Nipkow, E. Sekerinski (Eds.), FM 2006: Formal Methods. XV, 620 pages. 2006.

Vol. 4084: M.A. Wimmer, H.J. Scholl, Å. Grönlund, K.V. Andersen (Eds.), Electronic Government. XV, 353 pages. 2006.

Vol. 4083: S. Fischer-Hübner, S. Furnell, C. Lambrinoudakis (Eds.), Trust and Privacy in Digital Business. XIII, 243 pages. 2006.

Vol. 4082: K. Bauknecht, B. Pröll, H. Werthner (Eds.), E-Commerce and Web Technologies. XIII, 243 pages. 2006.

Vol. 4081: A. M. Tjoa, J. Trujillo (Eds.), Data Warehousing and Knowledge Discovery. XVII, 578 pages. 2006.

Vol. 4080: S. Bressan, J. Küng, R. Wagner (Eds.), Database and Expert Systems Applications. XXI, 959 pages. 2006.

Vol. 4079: S. Etalle, M. Truszczyński (Eds.), Logic Programming. XIV, 474 pages. 2006.

Vol. 4077: M.-S. Kim, K. Shimada (Eds.), Geometric Modeling and Processing - GMP 2006. XVI, 696 pages. 2006.

Vol. 4076: F. Hess, S. Pauli, M. Pohst (Eds.), Algorithmic Number Theory. X, 599 pages. 2006.

Vol. 4075: U. Leser, F. Naumann, B. Eckman (Eds.), Data Integration in the Life Sciences. XI, 298 pages. 2006. (Sublibrary LNBI).

Vol. 4074: M. Burmester, A. Yasinsac (Eds.), Secure Mobile Ad-hoc Networks and Sensors. X, 193 pages. 2006.

Vol. 4073: A. Butz, B. Fisher, A. Krüger, P. Olivier (Eds.), Smart Graphics. XI, 263 pages. 2006.

Vol. 4072: M. Harders, G. Székely (Eds.), Biomedical Simulation. XI, 216 pages. 2006.

Vol. 4071: H. Sundaram, M. Naphade, J.R. Smith, Y. Rui (Eds.), Image and Video Retrieval. XII, 547 pages. 2006.

Vol. 4070: C. Priami, X. Hu, Y. Pan, T.Y. Lin (Eds.), Transactions on Computational Systems Biology V. IX, 129 pages. 2006. (Sublibrary LNBI).

Vol. 4069: F.J. Perales, R.B. Fisher (Eds.), Articulated Motion and Deformable Objects. XV, 526 pages. 2006.

Vol. 4068: H. Schärfe, P. Hitzler, P. Øhrstrøm (Eds.), Conceptual Structures: Inspiration and Application. XI, 455 pages. 2006. (Sublibrary LNAI).

Vol. 4067: D. Thomas (Ed.), ECOOP 2006 – Object-Oriented Programming. XIV, 527 pages. 2006.

Vol. 4066: A. Rensink, J. Warmer (Eds.), Model Driven Architecture – Foundations and Applications. XII, 392 pages. 2006.

Vol. 4065: P. Perner (Ed.), Advances in Data Mining. XI, 592 pages. 2006. (Sublibrary LNAI).

Vol. 4064: R. Büschkes, P. Laskov (Eds.), Detection of Intrusions and Malware & Vulnerability Assessment. X, 195 pages. 2006.

Vol. 4063: I. Gorton, G.T. Heineman, I. Crnkovic, H.W. Schmidt, J.A. Stafford, C.A. Szyperski, K. Wallnau (Eds.), Component-Based Software Engineering. XI, 394 pages. 2006.

Vol. 4062: G. Wang, J.F. Peters, A. Skowron, Y. Yao (Eds.), Rough Sets and Knowledge Technology. XX, 810 pages. 2006. (Sublibrary LNAI).

Vol. 4061: K. Miesenberger, J. Klaus, W. Zagler, A.I. Karshmer (Eds.), Computers Helping People with Special Needs. XXIX, 1356 pages. 2006.